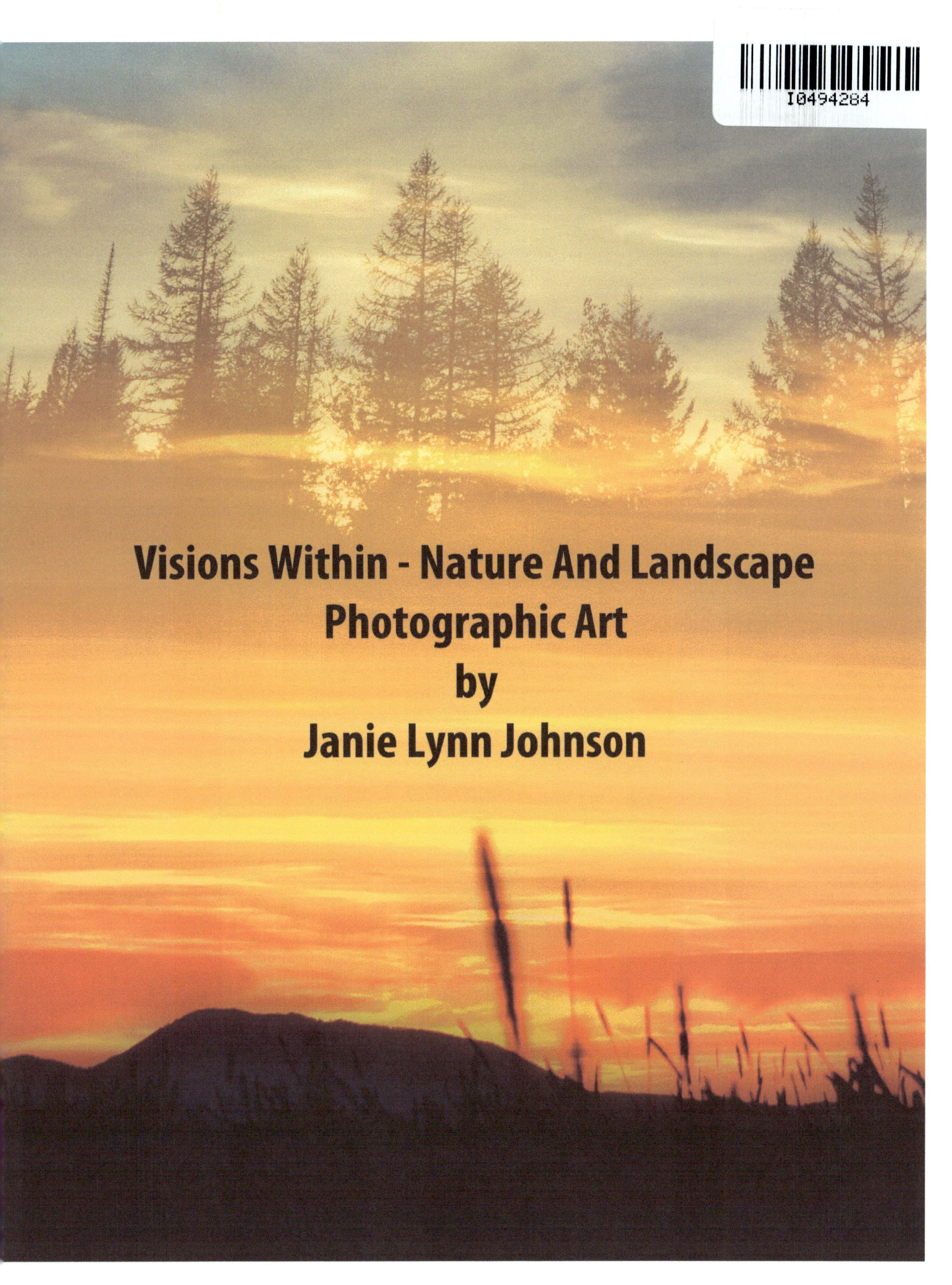

Visions Within - Nature And Landscape Photographic Art
by
Janie Lynn Johnson

For information about custom editions, special sales, signings, premium, and corporate purchases please contact:

Publisher: Sound Impressions

Address: Sound Impressions
            Attn: Publishing
            PO Box 754
            Boonton, NJ 07005

Phone: (973) – 263 – 0521

Web: http://www.storystick.com

Produced By: Jason Koba

Photographs by: Janie Lynn Johnson

A Note From The Artist

This is my second and hopefully not my last book. As those who have seen my first book will see, I've done things differently with this one.

A lot has happened in my life since my first book (The Eye Behind The Lense). My family and I have experienced some significant losses in that time. I had no desire to create for a time, but I have grown as a person and my work now has more meaning personally. I look at things differently now. However, one thing that remains the same is my staying true to how I edit and compose a collage through manipulation. Emotions, smells, memories, and how the day feels to me, plays a huge part in my editing of my images. Editing for me is my paintbrush and canvas. I can create in any way I choose.

The images I have included in this book were chosen based on my experiences over the last year. The groupings are about friendships made, experiences had, and moving on. With that note, I would like to dedicate this book to my best friend (who is no longer with us), my new friends, as well as my long lasting friends (one of whom is publisher of this book), and as always, those members of my family who have been supportive. You know who you are. Your support means so much to me. I know I wouldn't have made it this far without all of you.

'Peace And Serenity'

'Pride' - When all the color is gone and one if left standing- holding pride in the beauty of what life is meant to be.

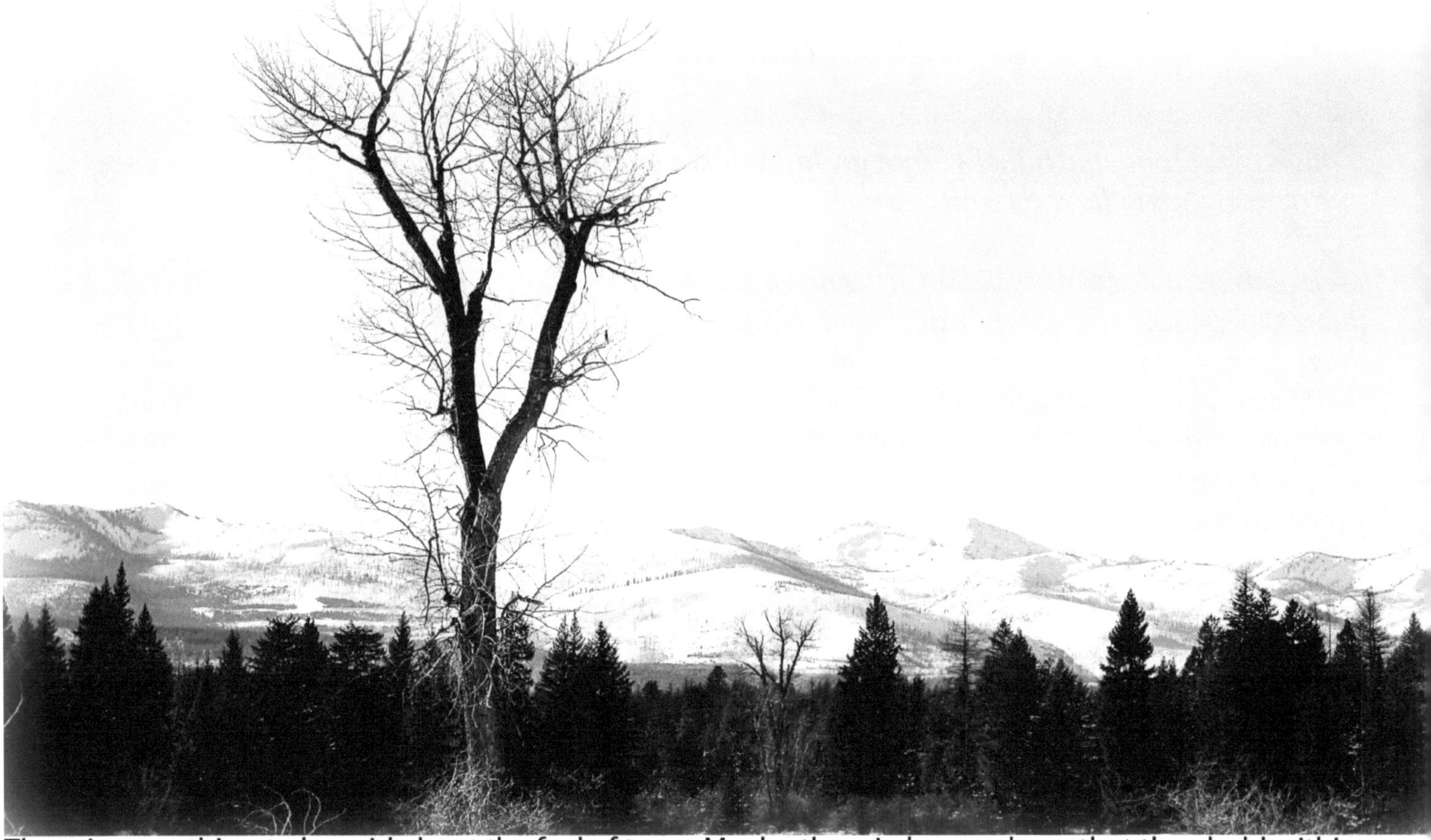

There is something to be said about the feel of trees. Maybe the wisdom and age that they hold within. Whether in black and white or color, I love a good tree scene. The stories they tell.   -Montana

'Trees In The Mist'

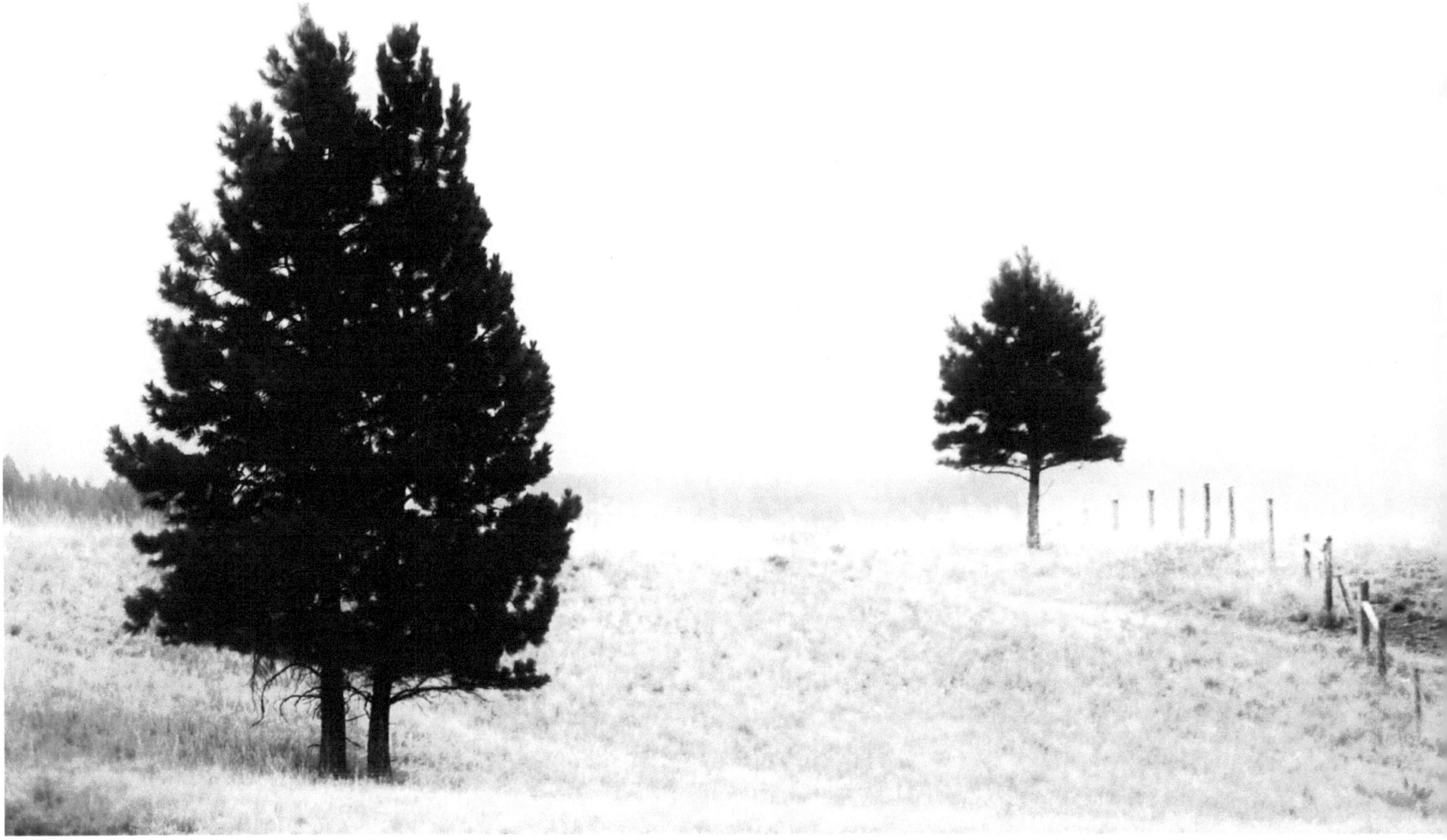

"Dreaming Of Aspens" 2015 - Montana - Jocko Lakes area

Morrell Falls - Seeley Lake, Montana 2015

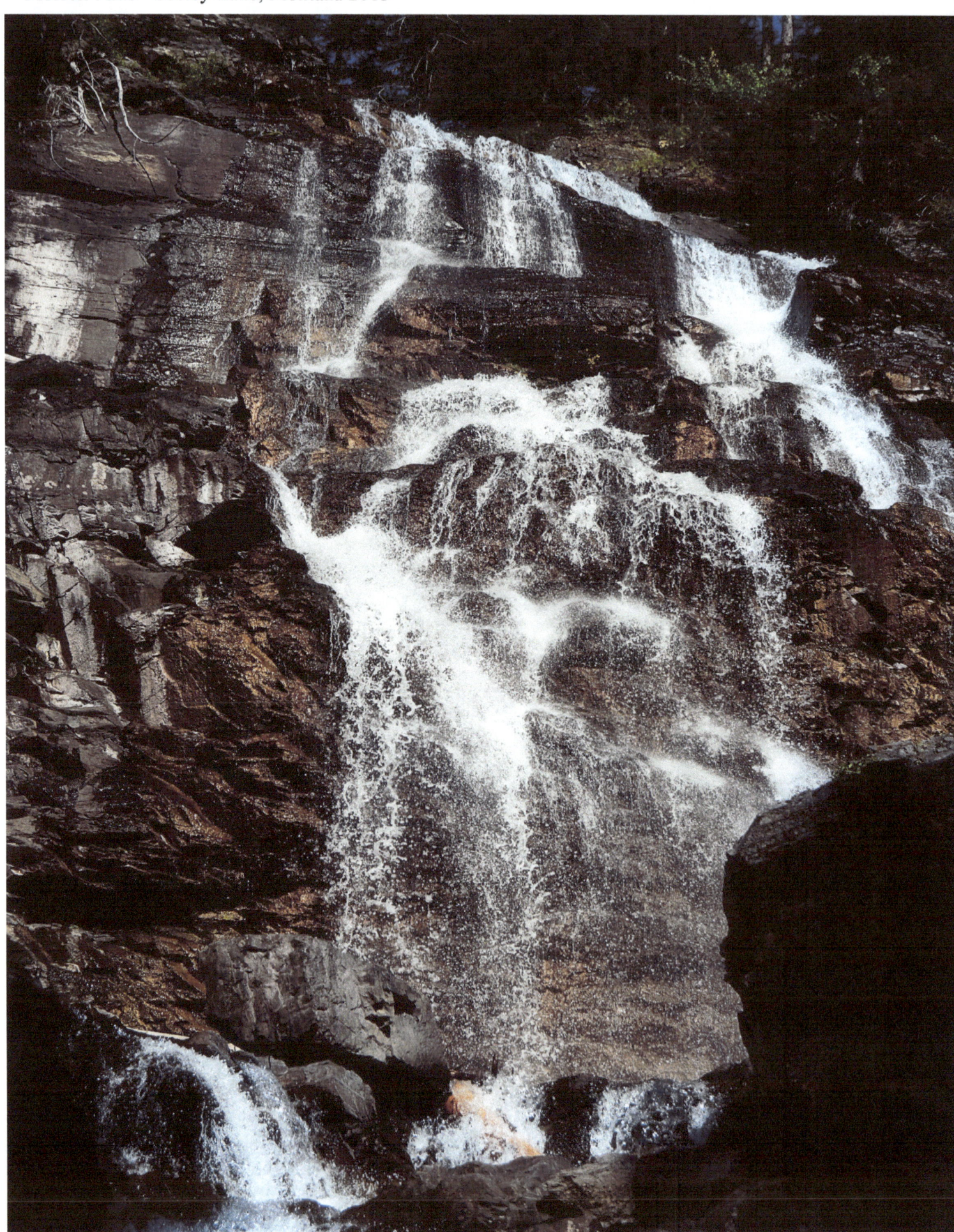

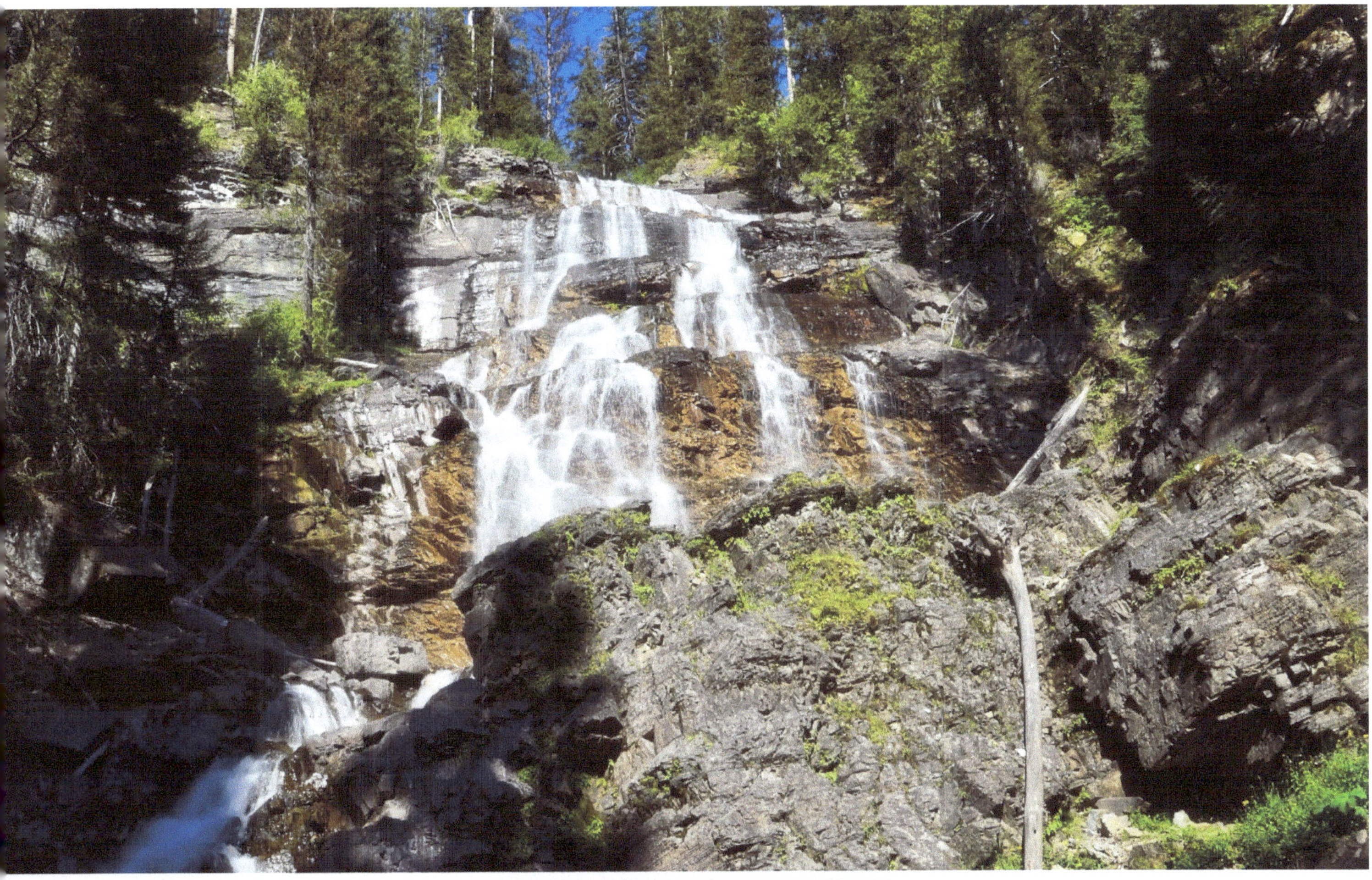

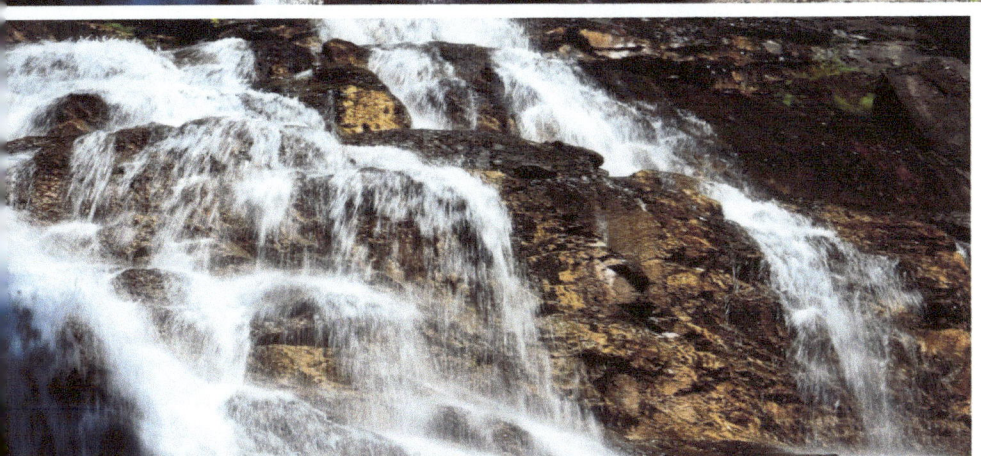

Morrell Falls - Seeley Lake,
Montana 2015

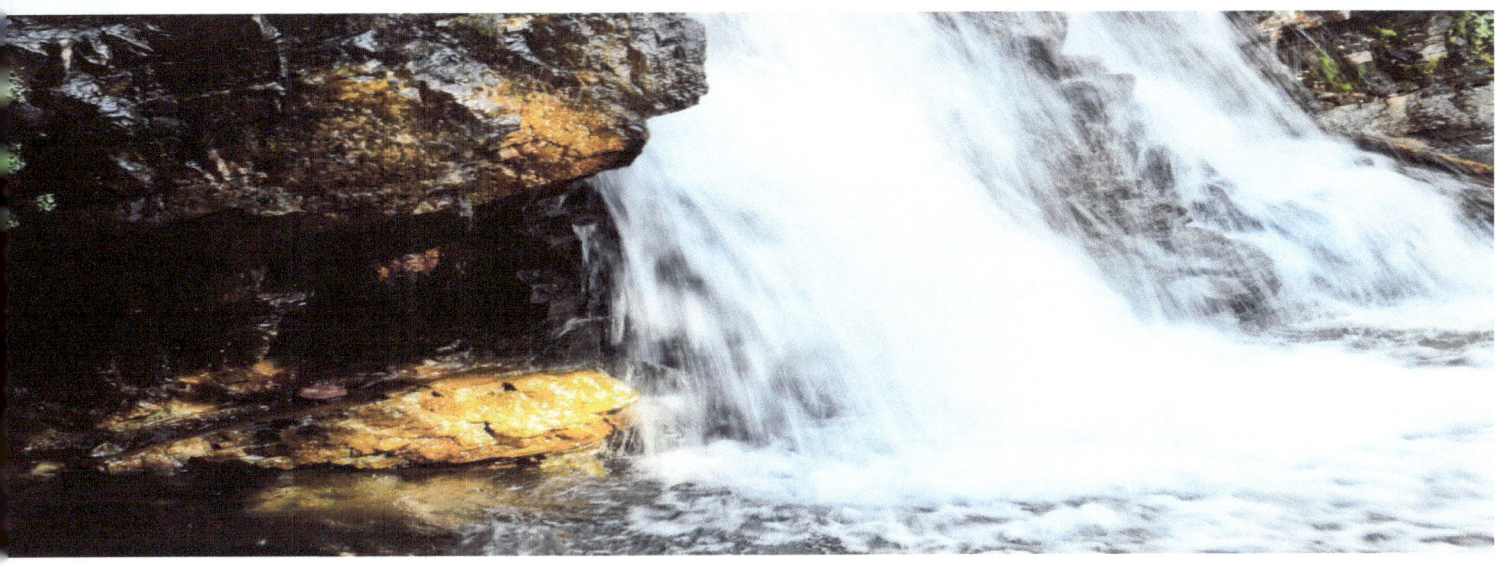

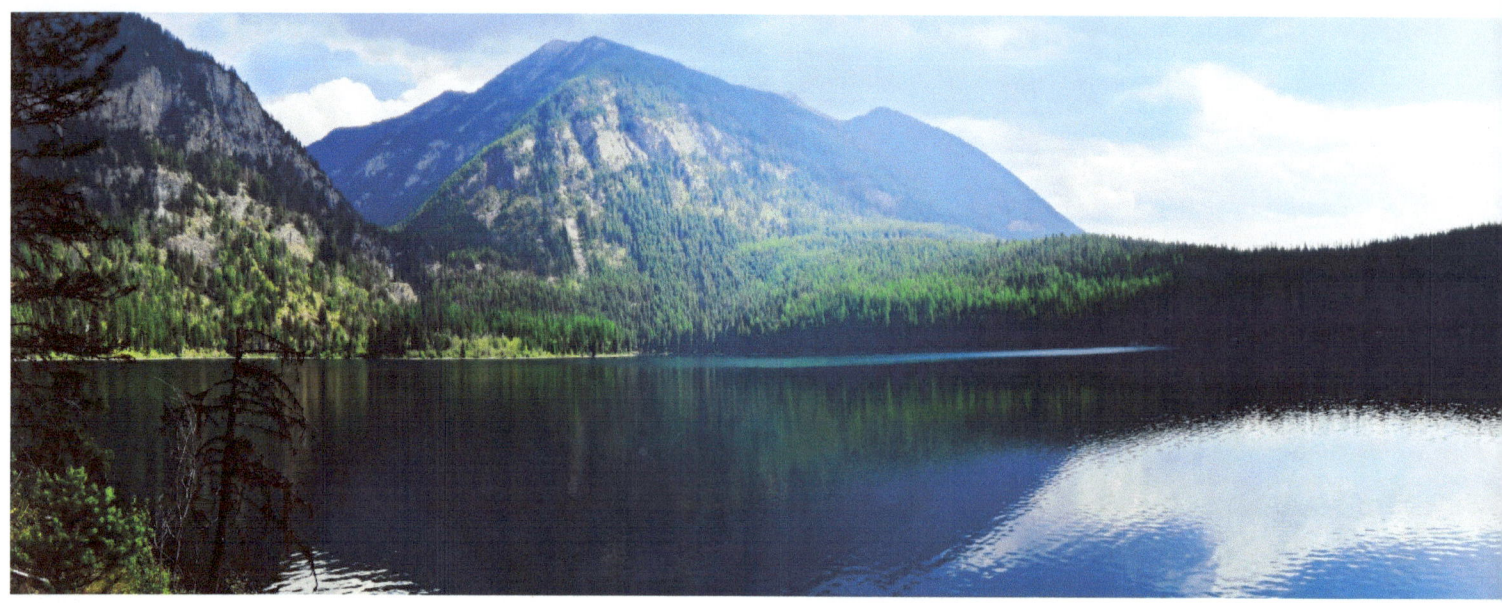

Above - The view on the hike up to Holland Falls. The falls are between the two mountains. A stunning site. Holland Lake, Montana 2015

Below - Another view in black and white while standing on a little peninsula on the shore behind a small island nestled in the lake. So many views - Holland Lake, Montana 2015

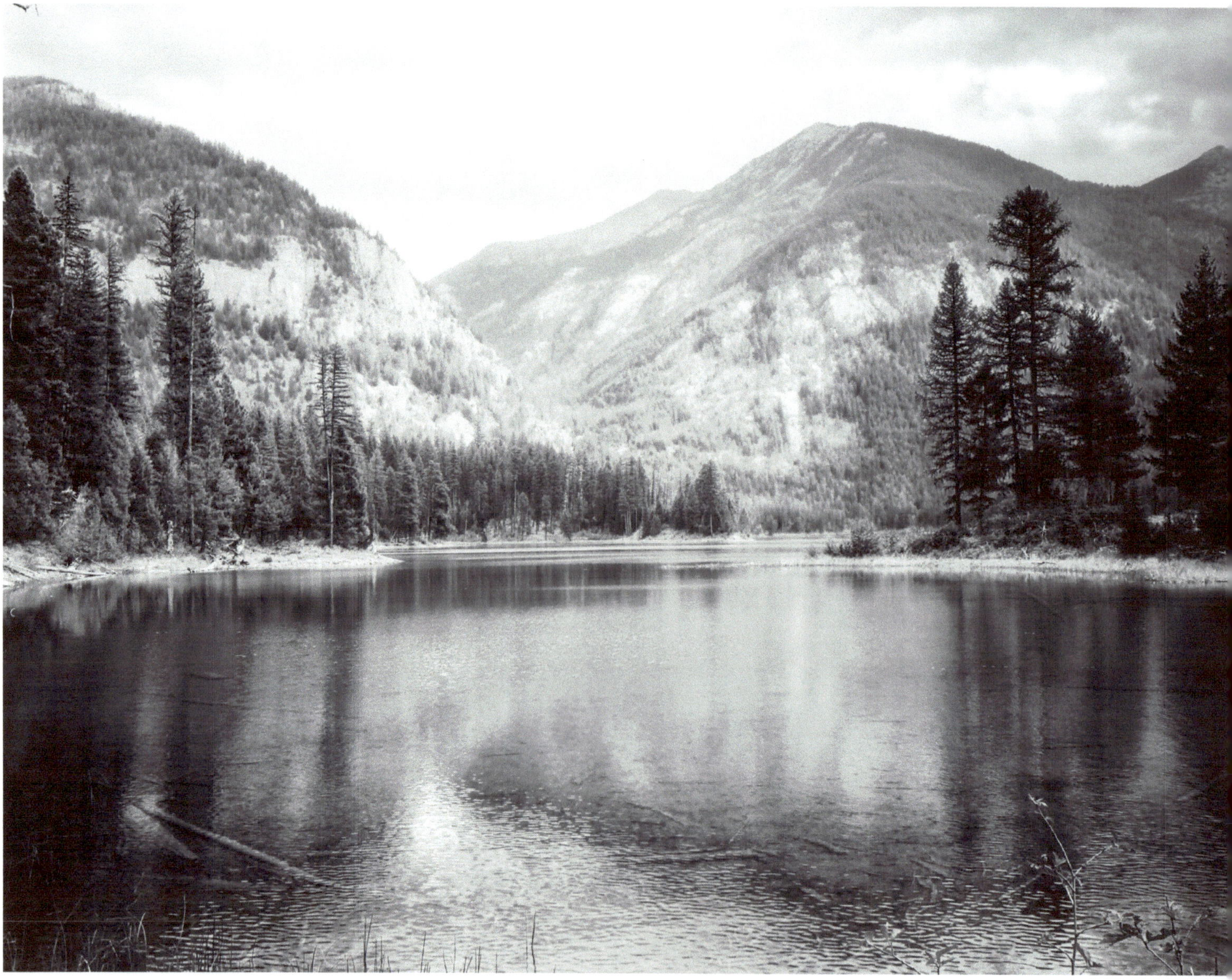

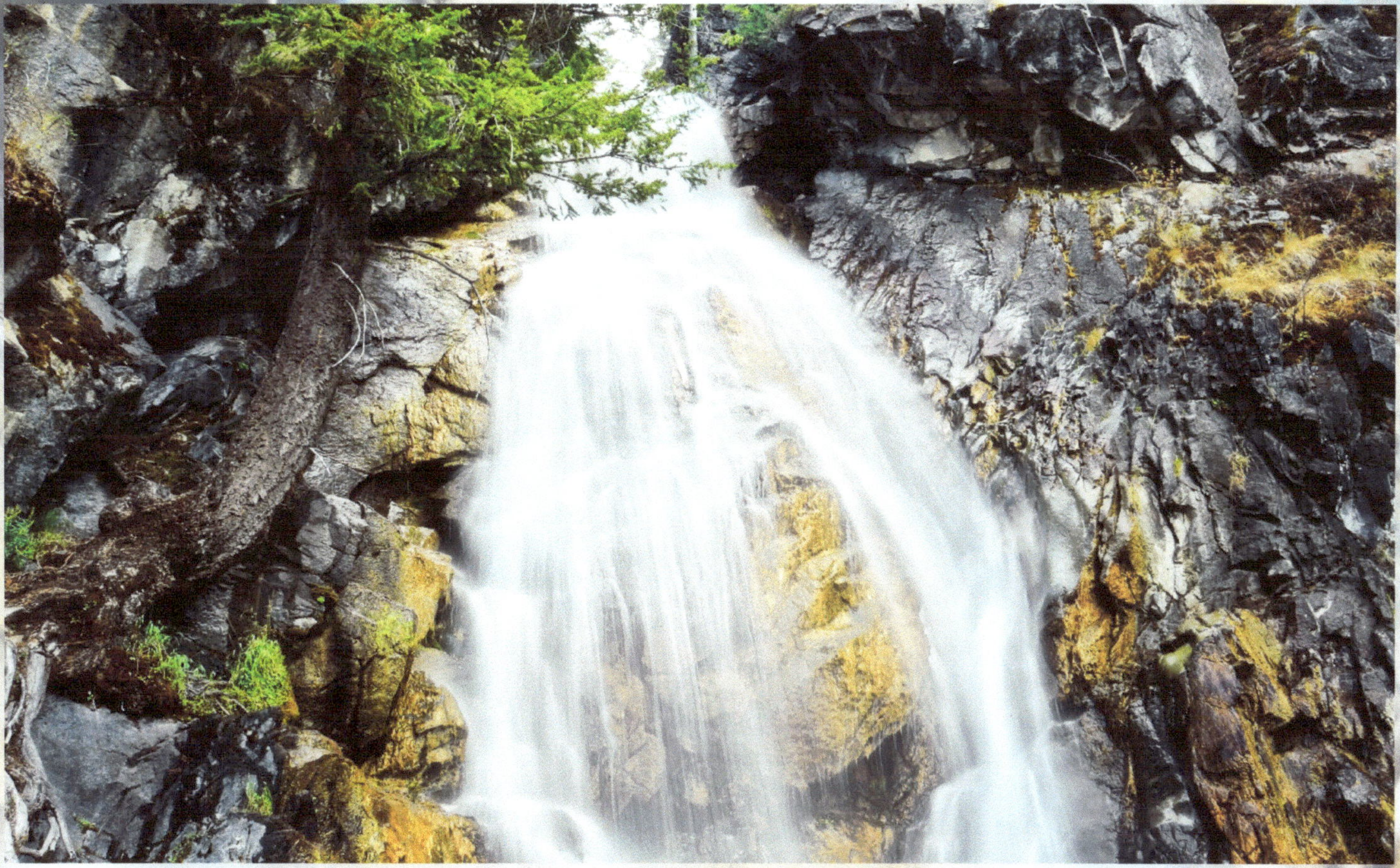

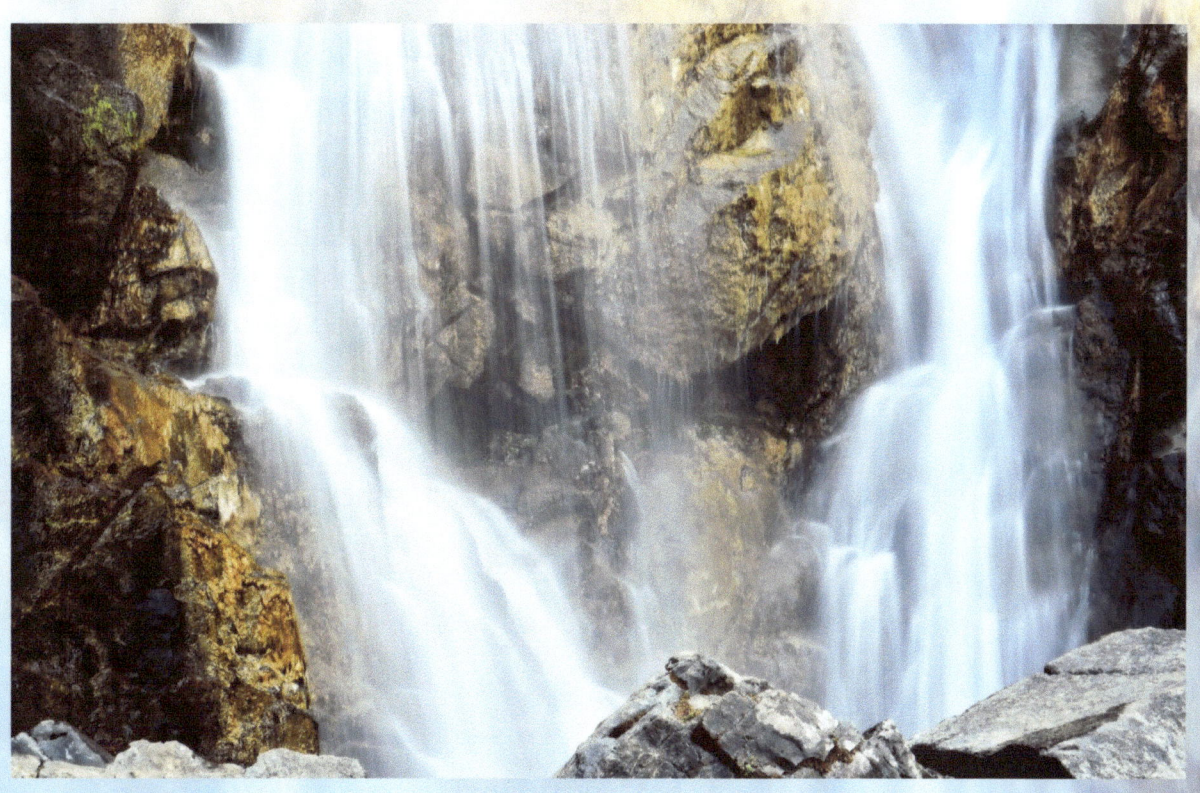

We have reached our destination - Holland Falls. The beauty of it was definitely a truth. So glad I got the opportunity to view this on such a perfect day. If you look close, it looks like the rock behind the falls have evil eyes!

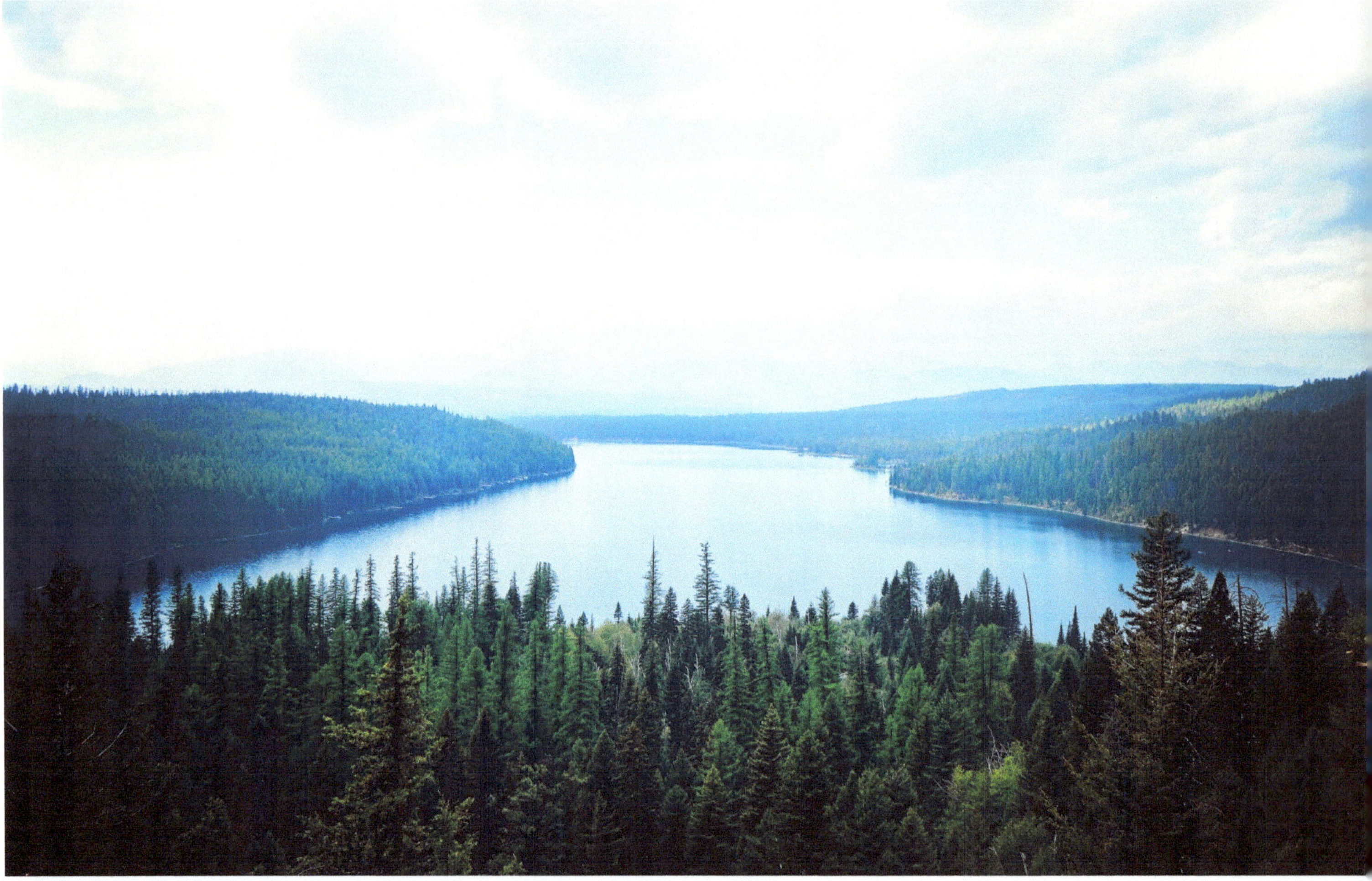

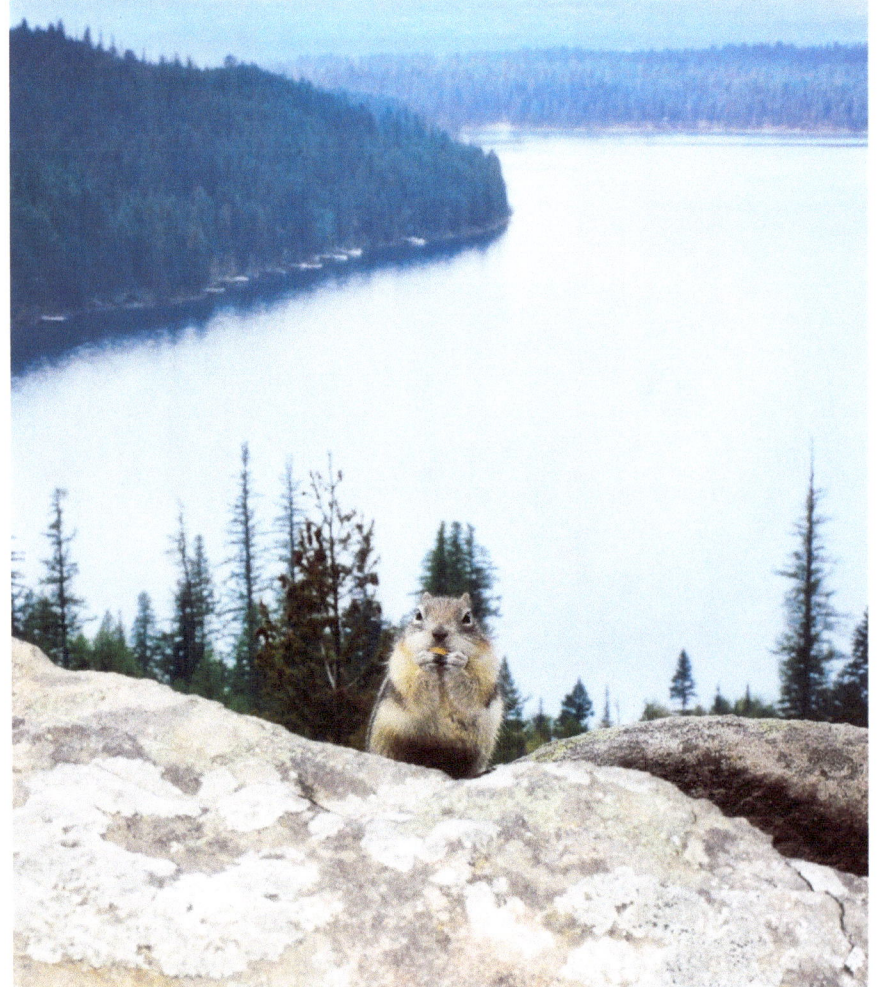

**Above Holland Lake, Montana
2015**

Here we are at the tip of the path, making our way back down. The view was beautiful. The image above I named 'Companionship' . Companionship of nature as well as good company.

To the left -'On Top Of The World' is a portrait of a sweet little chipmunk we called Alvin.

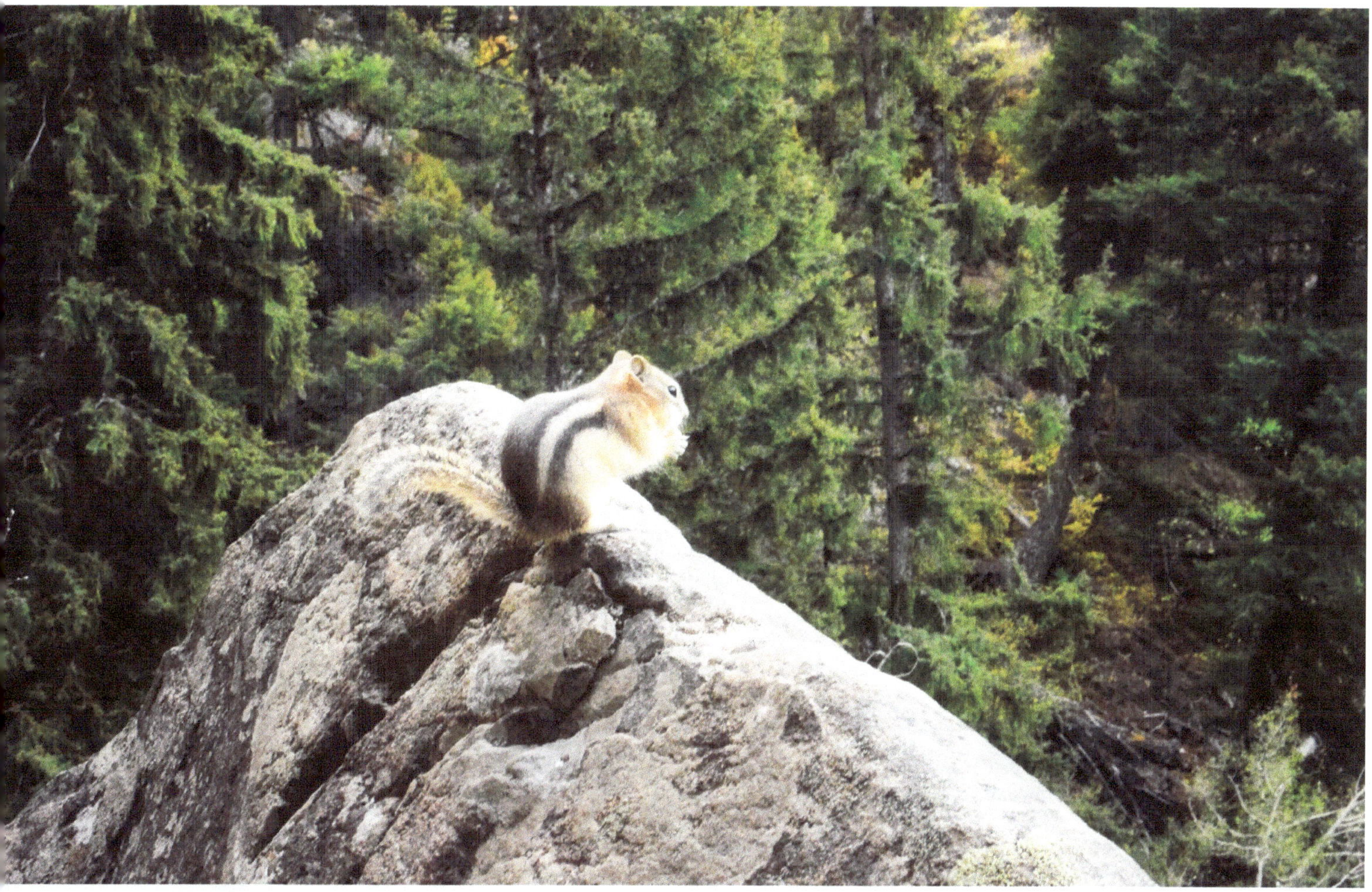

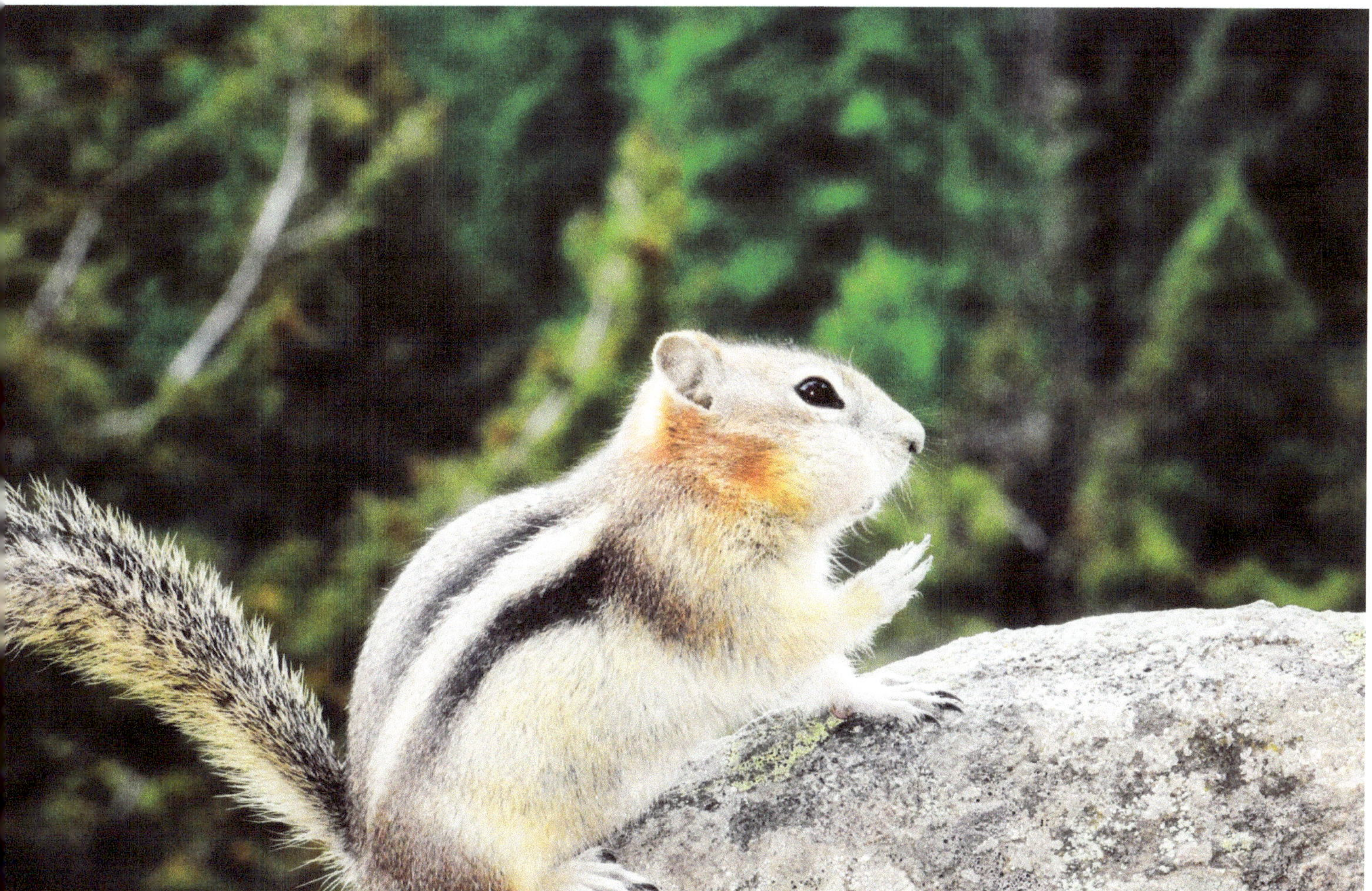

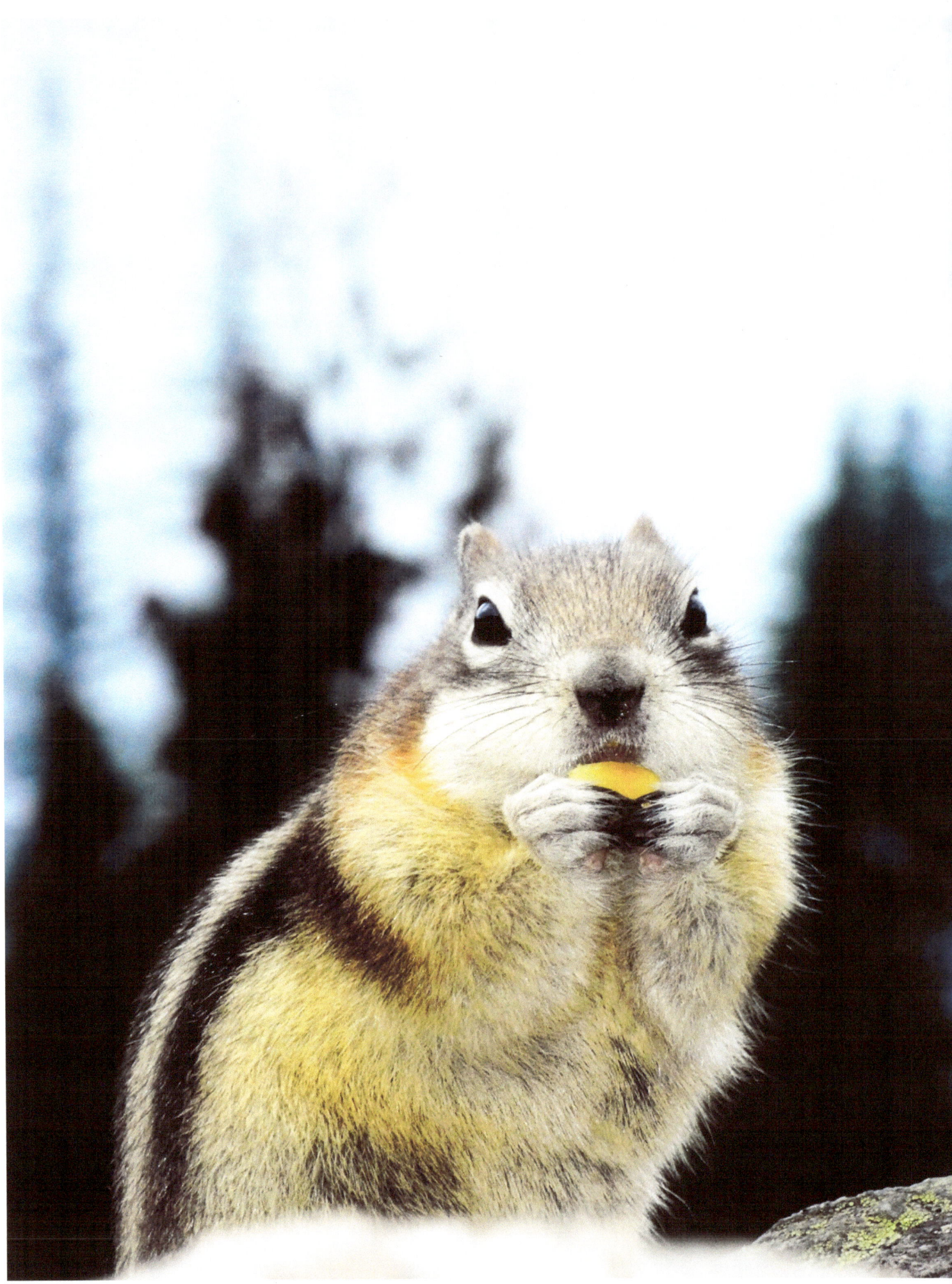

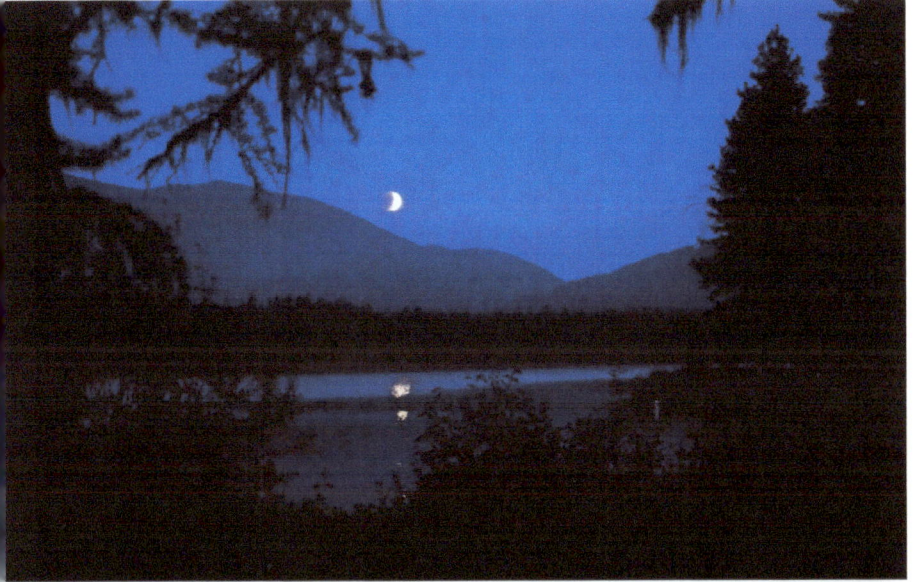

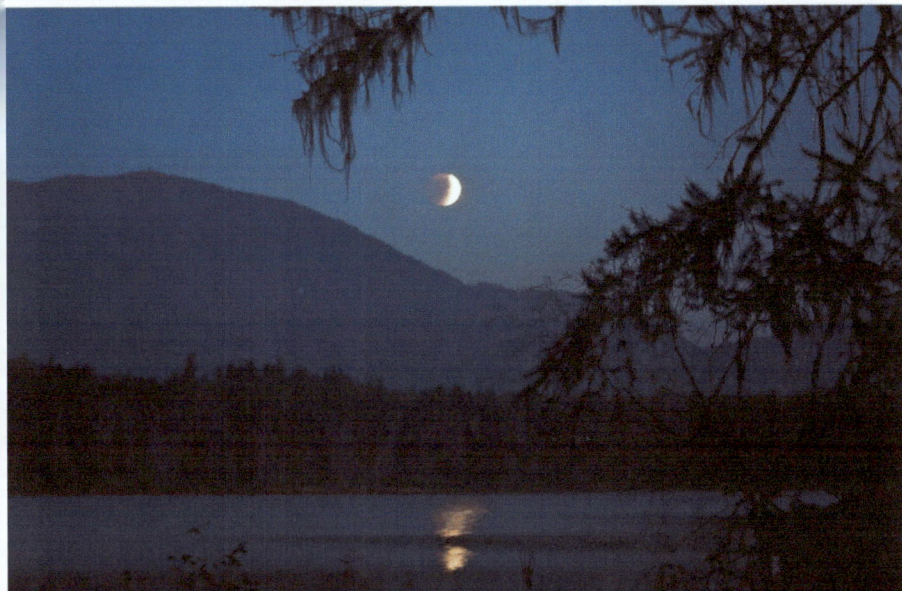

In 2015 a rare event occured. The Super Blood Moon Lunar Eclipse. The evening of September 27, hoping for clear skies , my friend and I searched for an ideal spot to capture this moment. I was very proud of the captures that I had gotten, as I have had little practice shooting the moon. Going by the calculations from start to finish times, this is the set that I captured before I was getting so tired. We started on the shores of Seeley Lake and finished it up off my back porch. The night was getting very chilly. I was grateful I had a good friend to have fun with. The less thinking about trying to get a good shot tends to help me get a good shot.

 I hope you enjoy the display I captured on this night and a huge thank you to my best friend. I dedicate these images to her son who would have had just as much of a good time capturing this moment as we did.

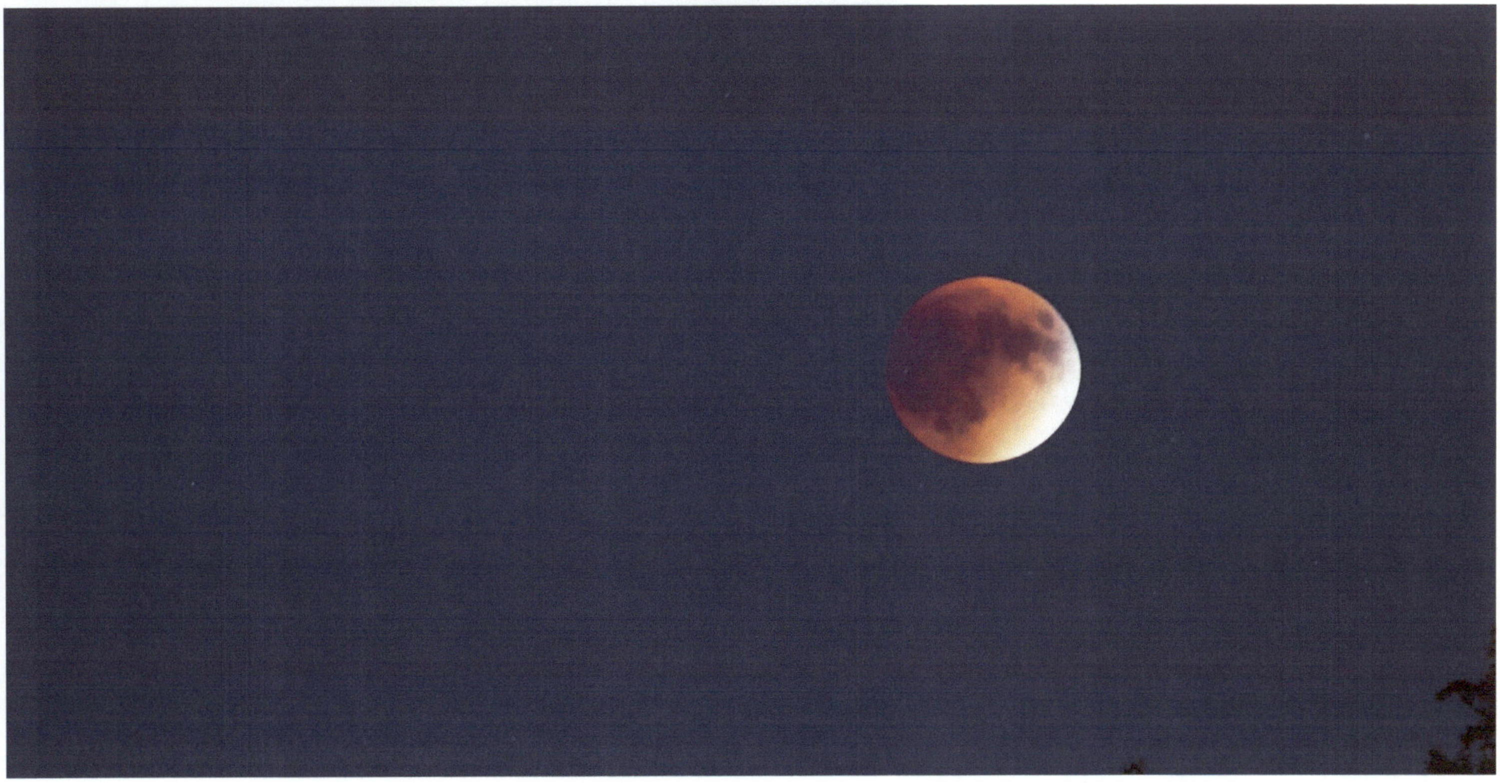

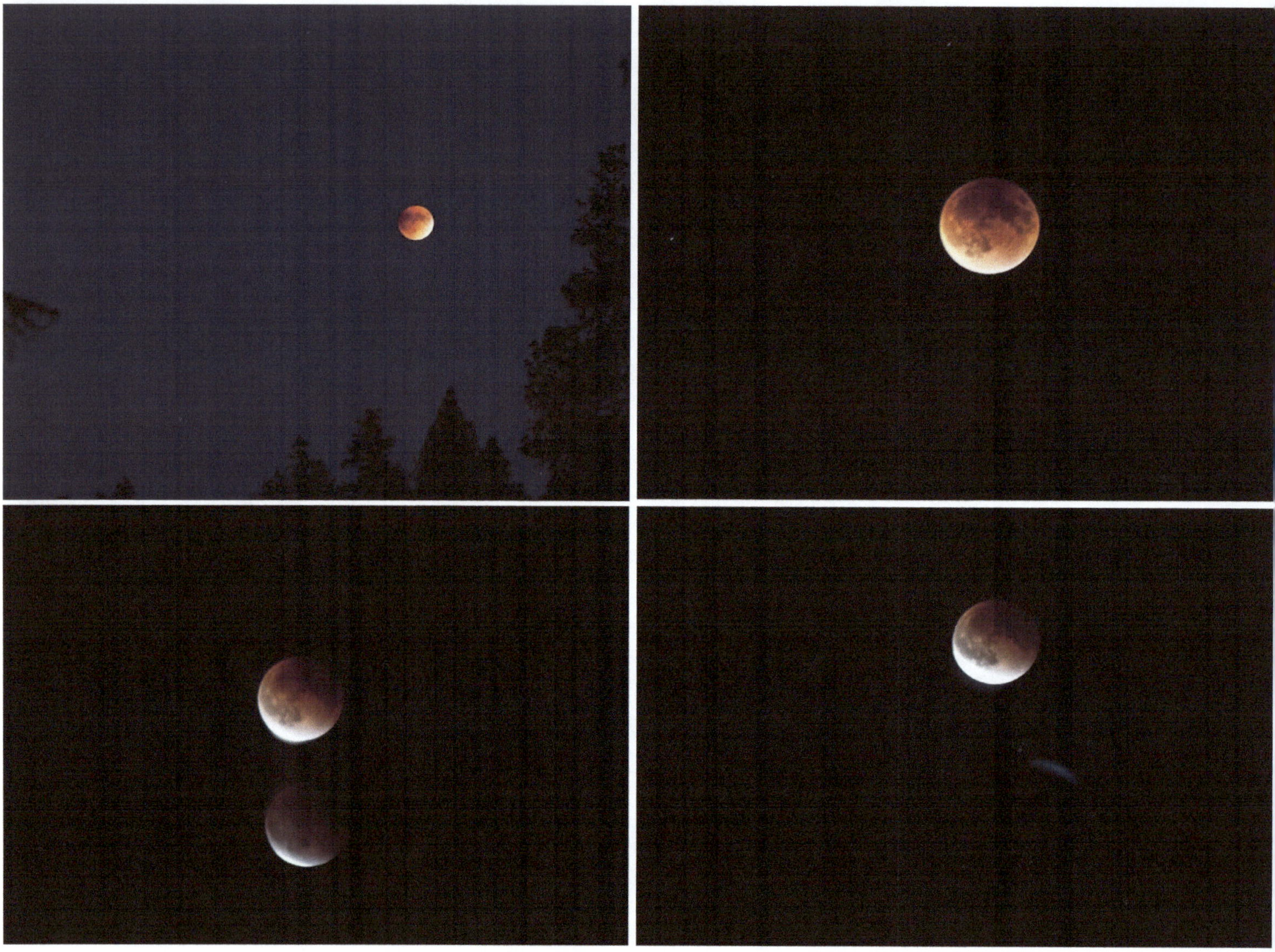

In the two images directly above, I was playing with a little movement on the tripod. We are nearing the end of the eclipse. *Super Blood Moon Lunar Eclipse - September 2015 in Seeley Lake, Montana*

National Bison Range - Montana - September 2015. *'Pristine Panoramic View'*

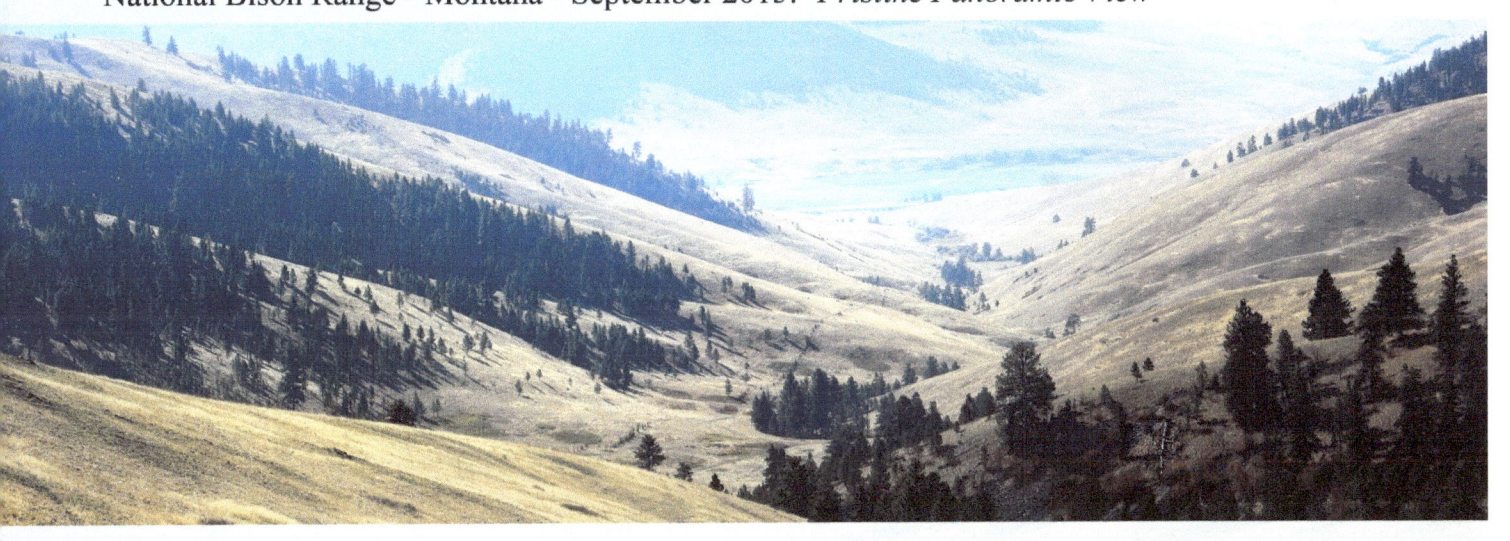

At the top lookout area facing the Mission Mountain Range. A little photo distortion with my edit.

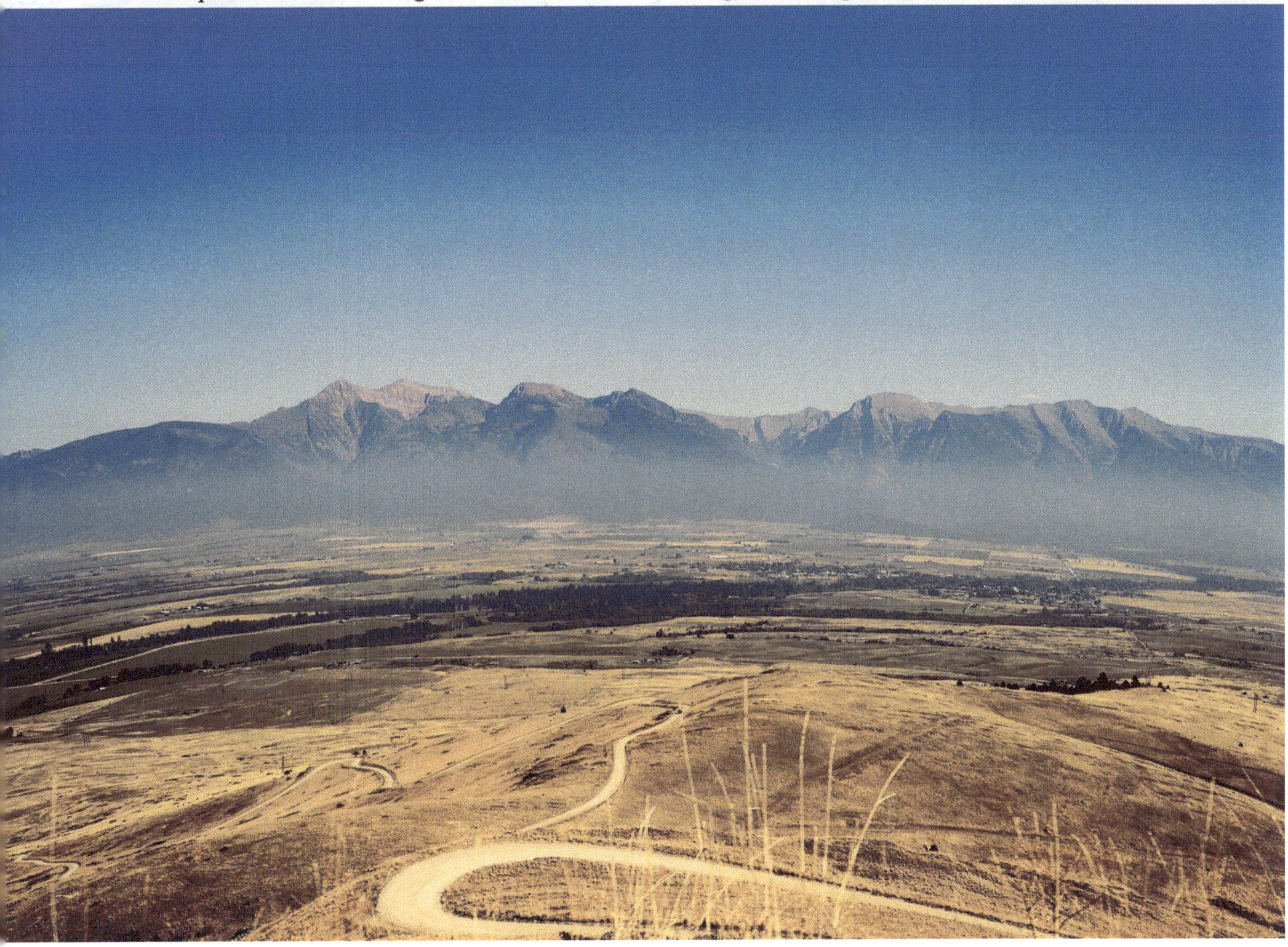

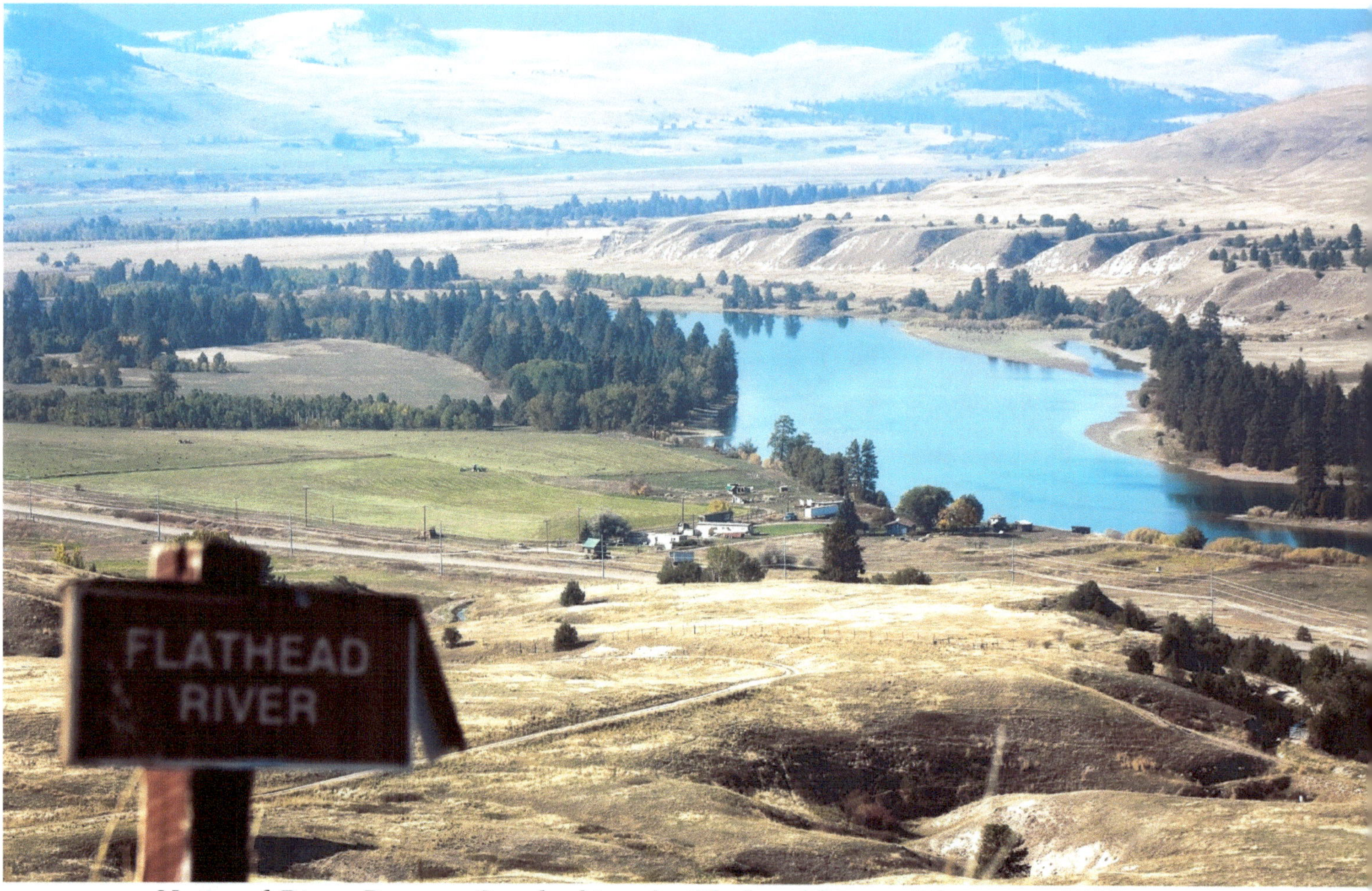

National Bison Range - Overlooking the Flathead River. Montana - 2015

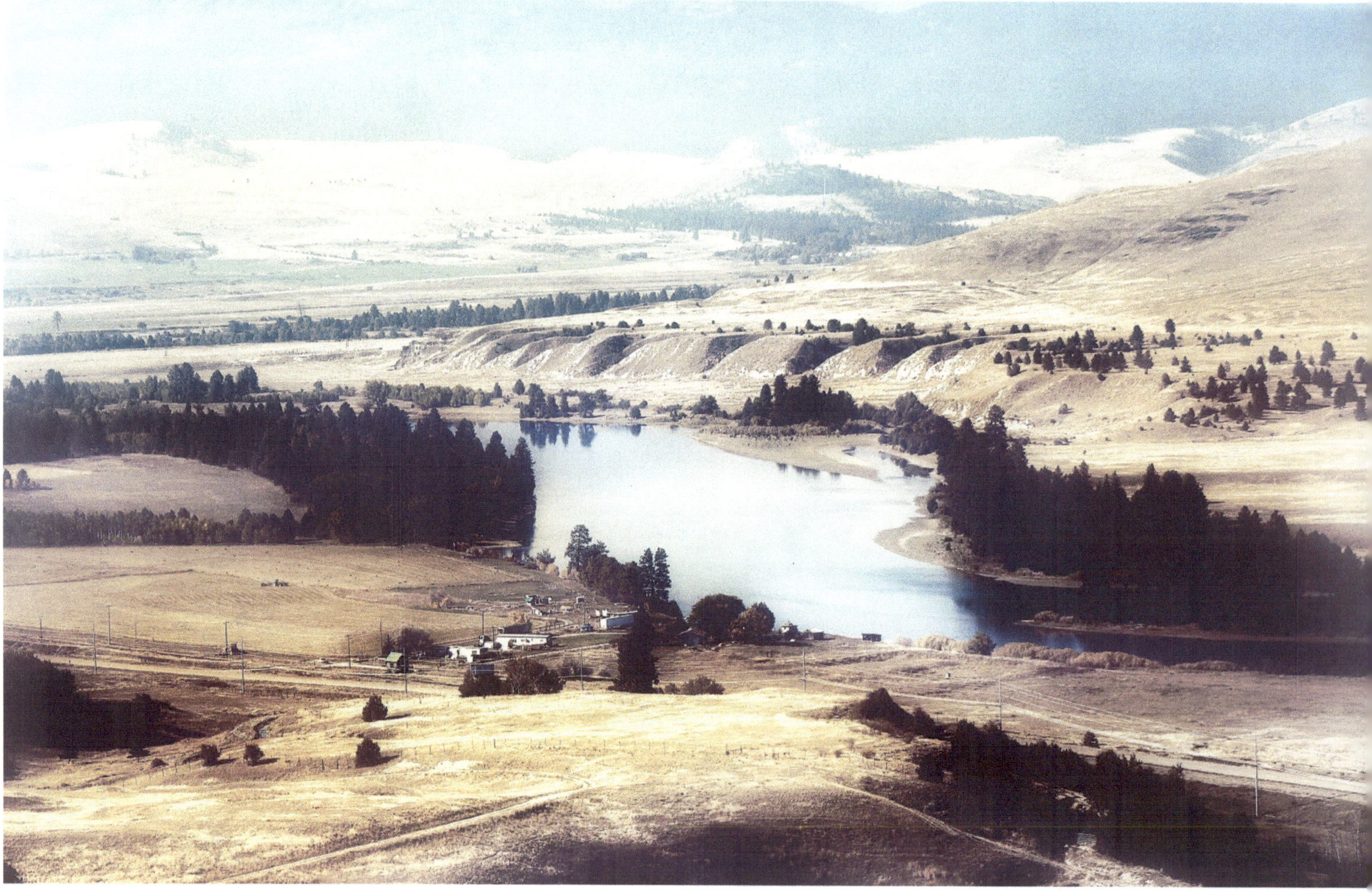

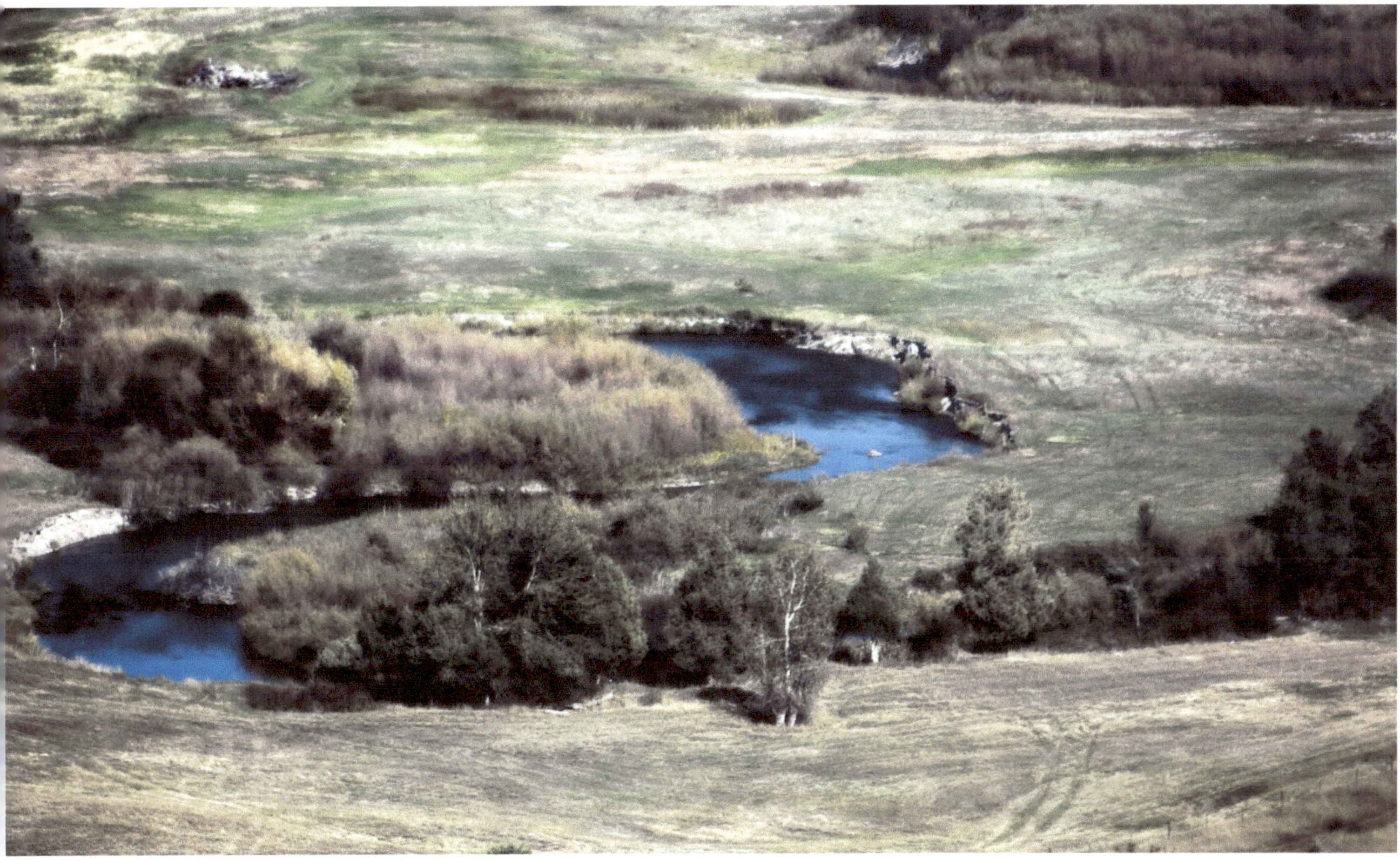

Different shots of the Flathead River both taken with 3 exposures each and merged together to create a high dynamic range image - *National Bison Range - Montana 2015*

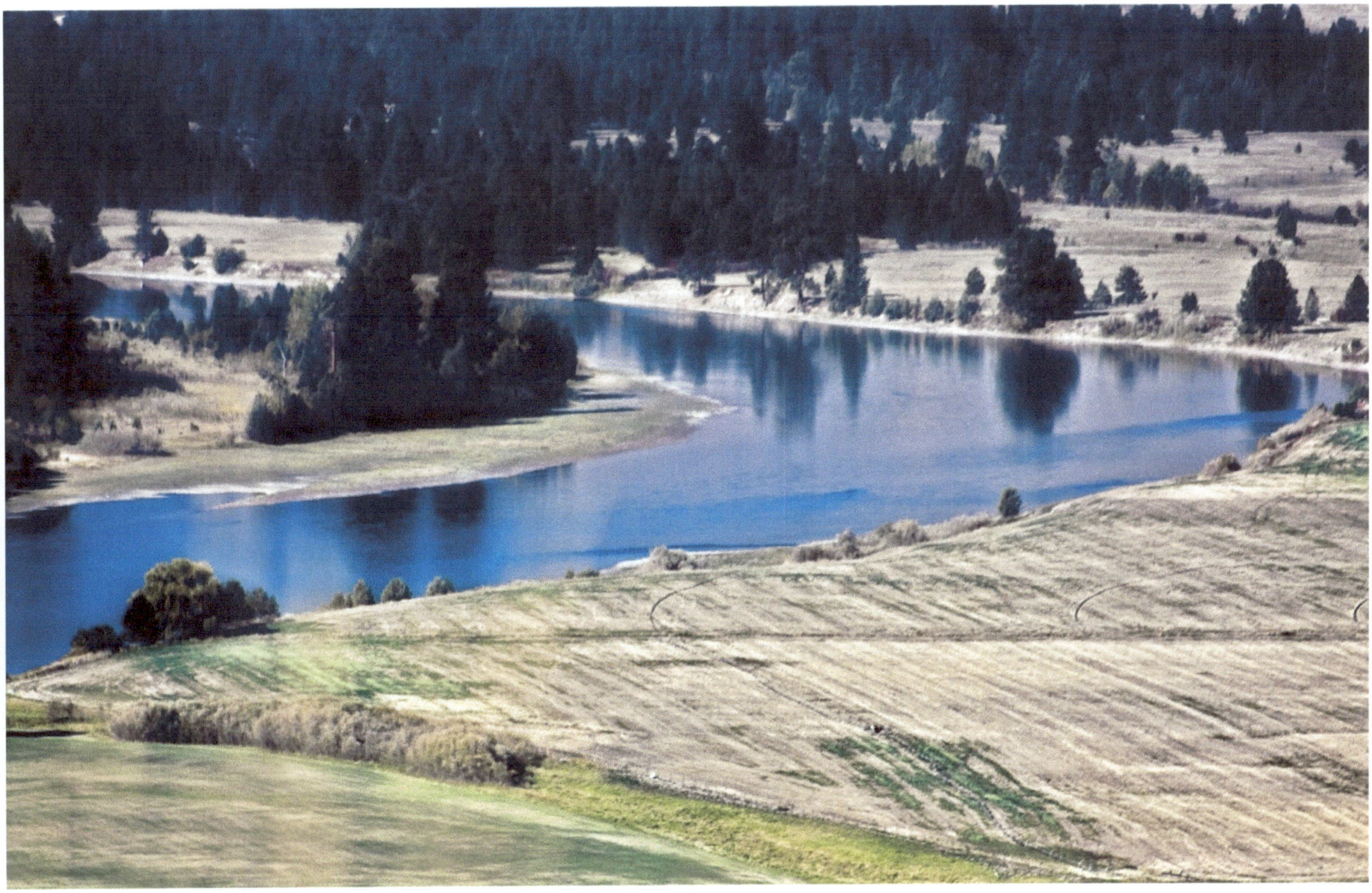

'Lonely Bison' - National Bison Range- Montana 2015

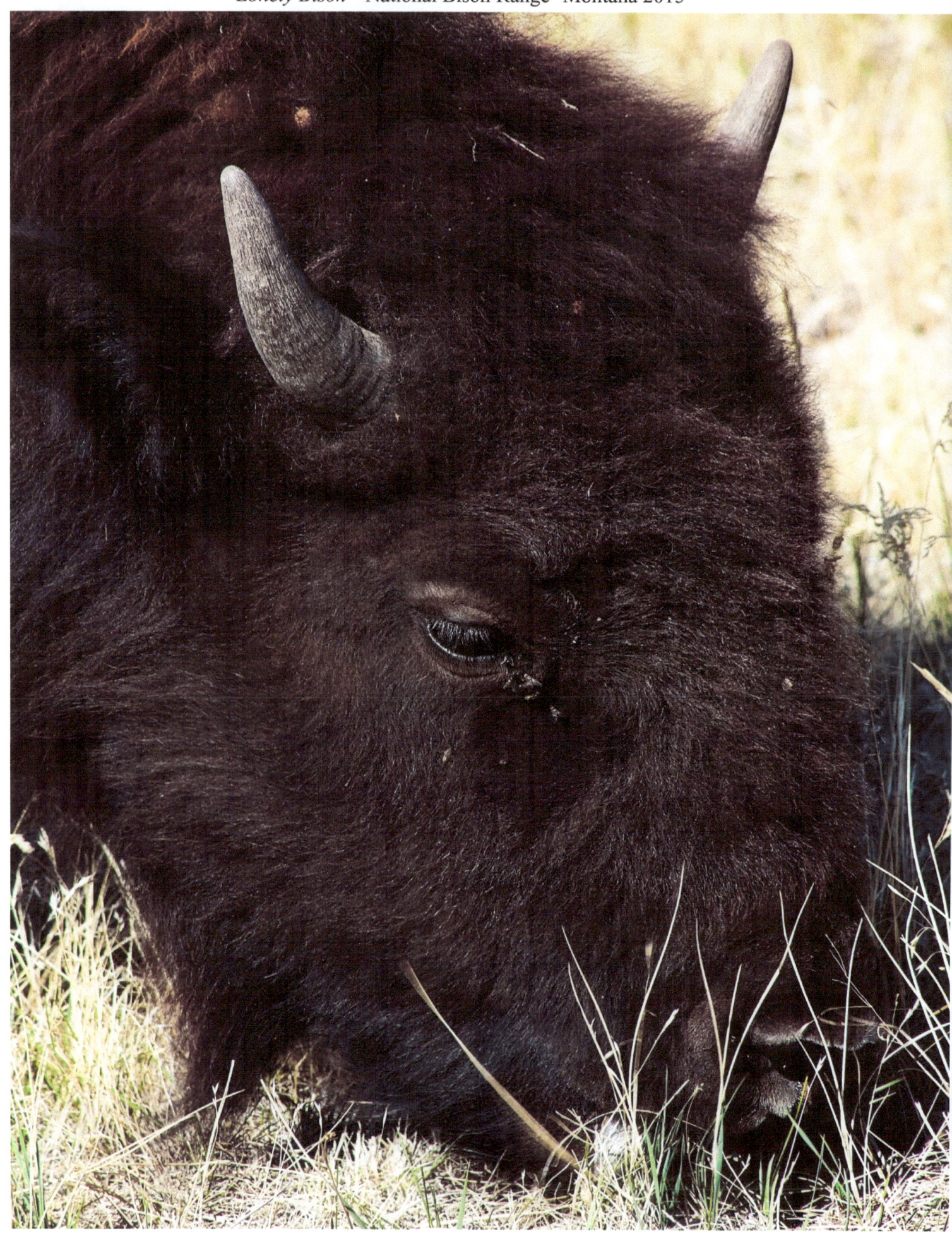

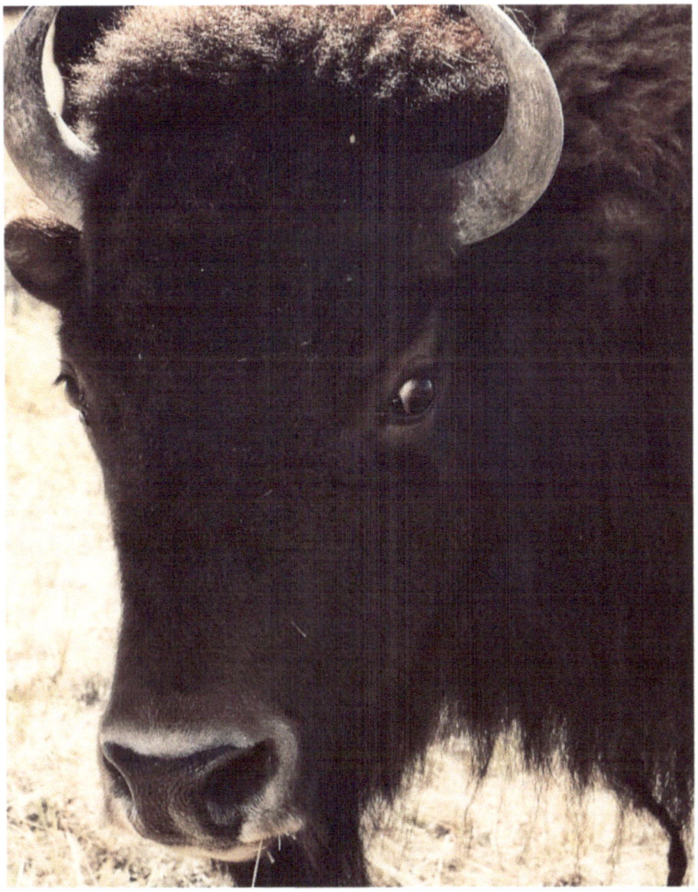

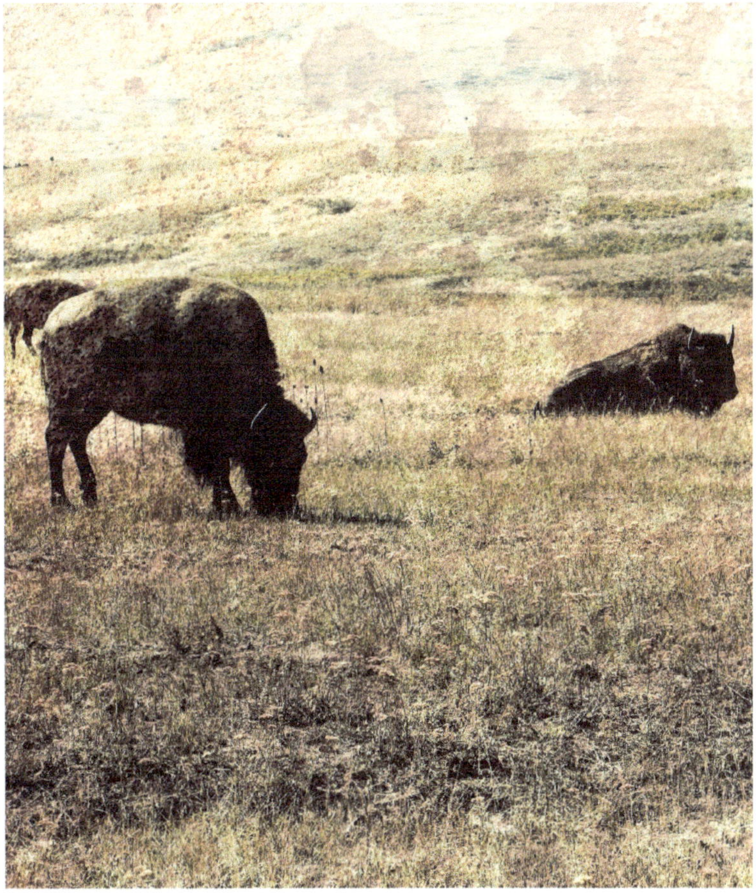

'Home On The Range' - Below we were able to get the chance to see the Bison round-up happening throughout the park today. Men on horses and 4-wheelers herding them down the hills.

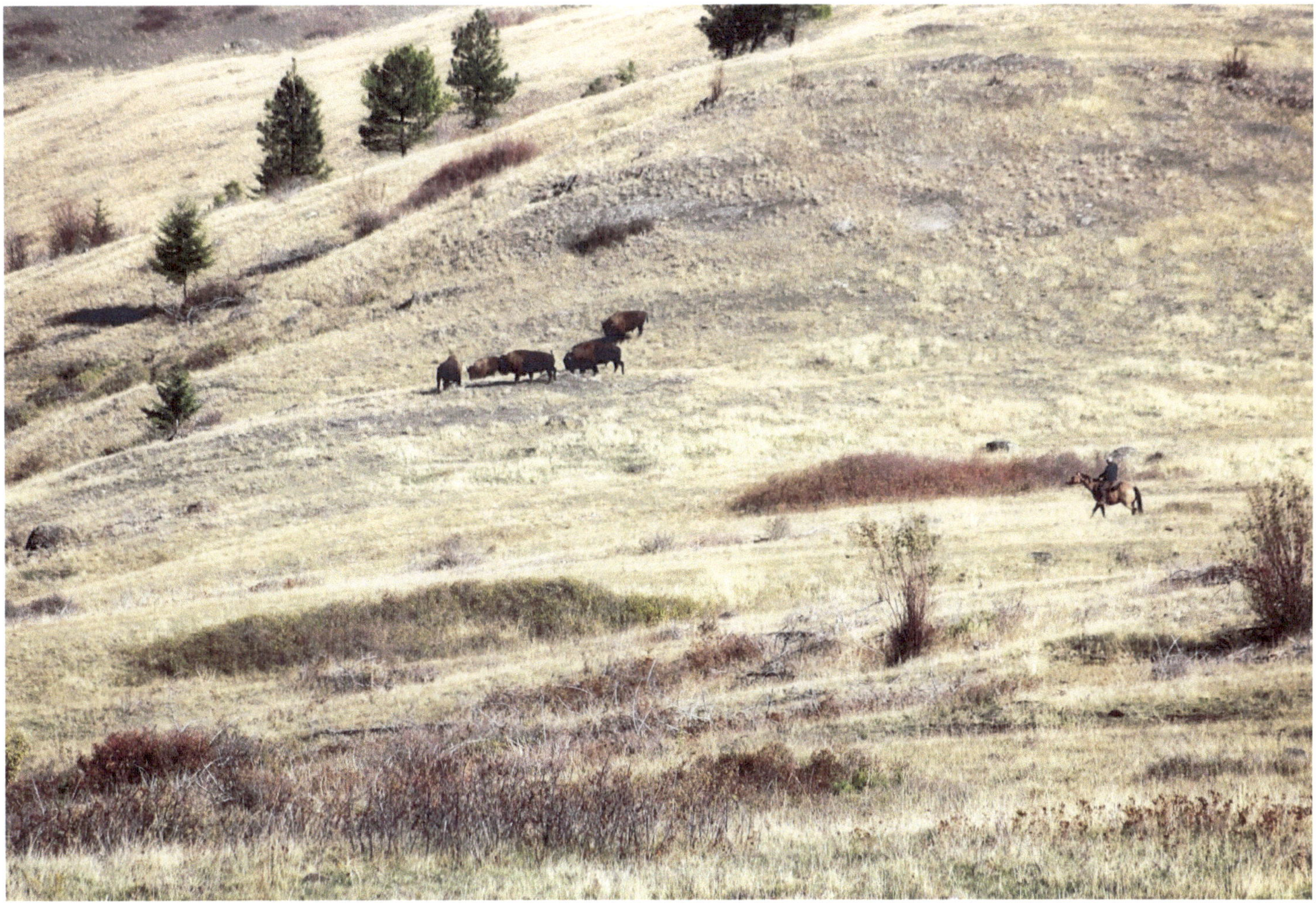

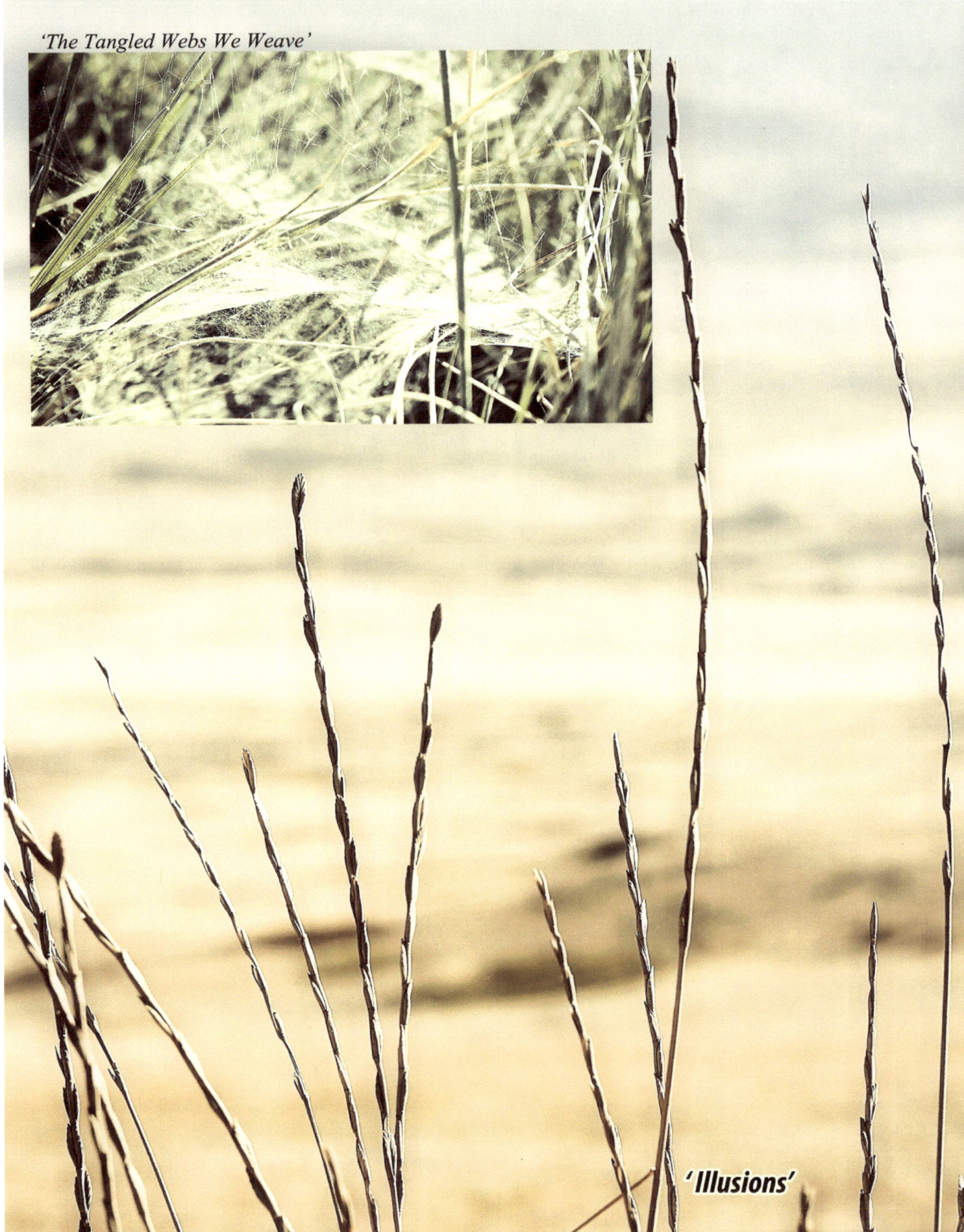

'The Tangled Webs We Weave'

'Illusions'

A cute little spring falling from the above mountain on this cool autumn evening before the sun goes down. We are on our way back to Seeley Lake from the National Bison Range. Jocko Lakes area -Montana.

'Dreamy Autumn Spring '

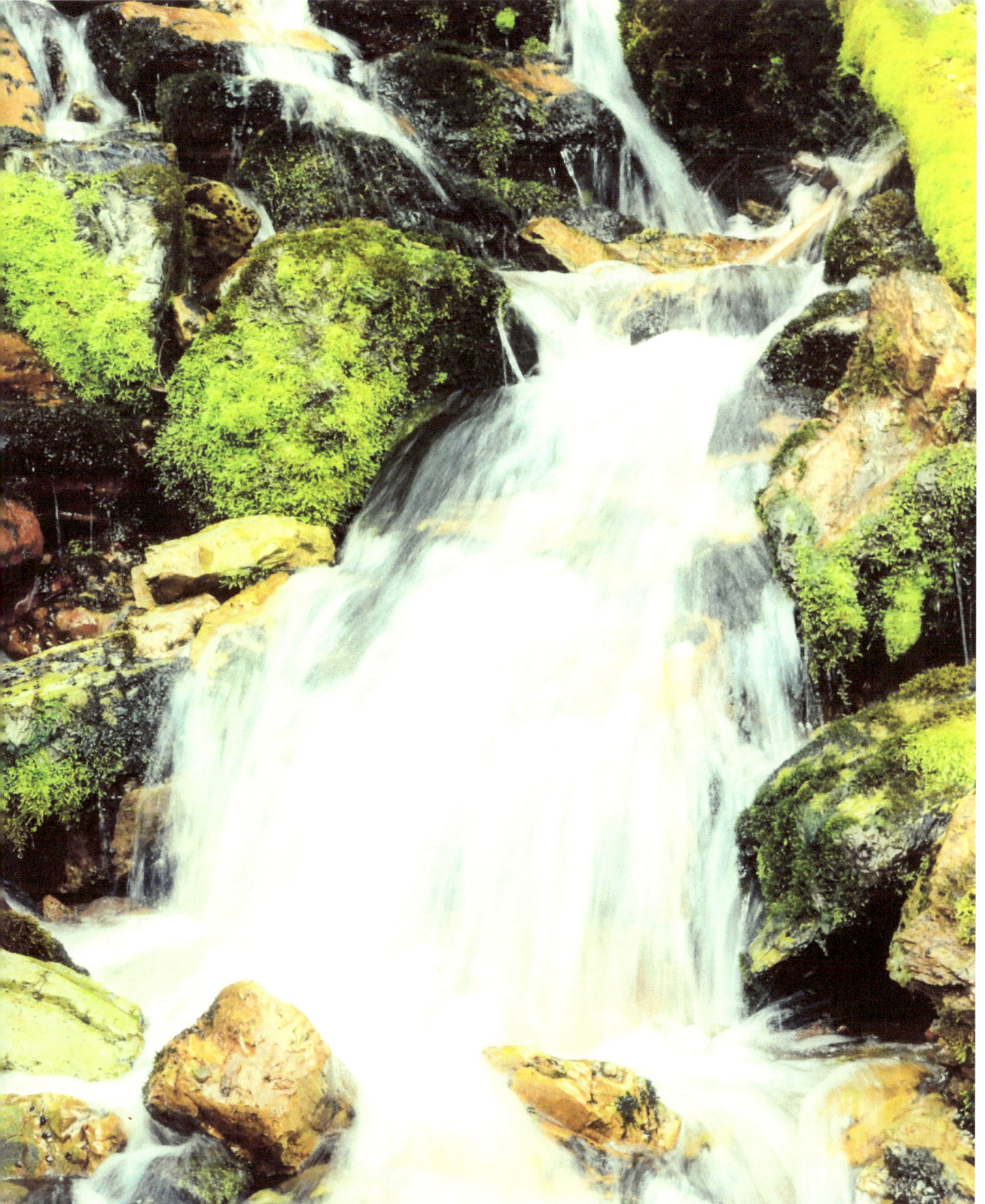

Newport Bridge- Newport, Oregon - 2015

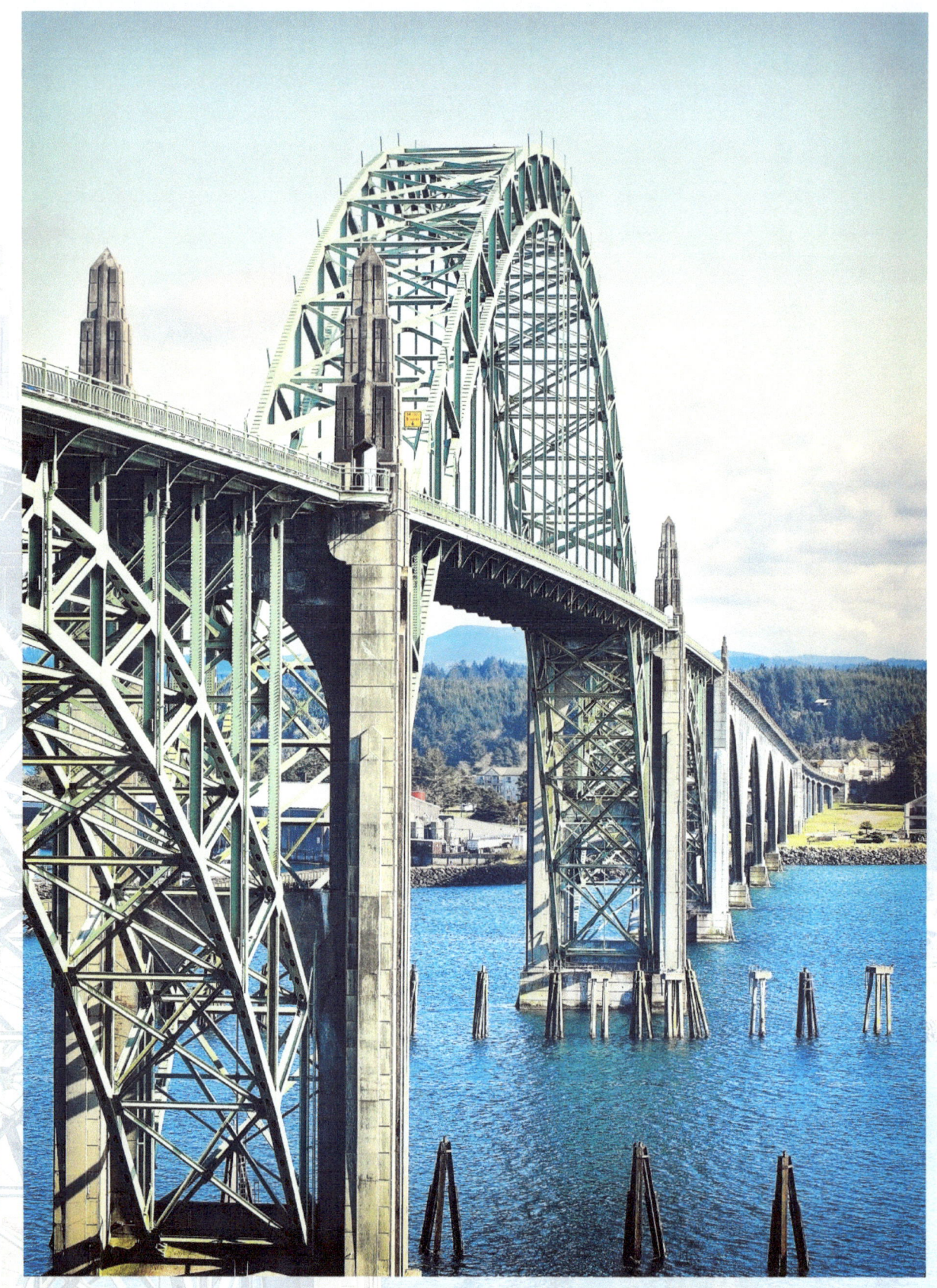

'A New Perspective'

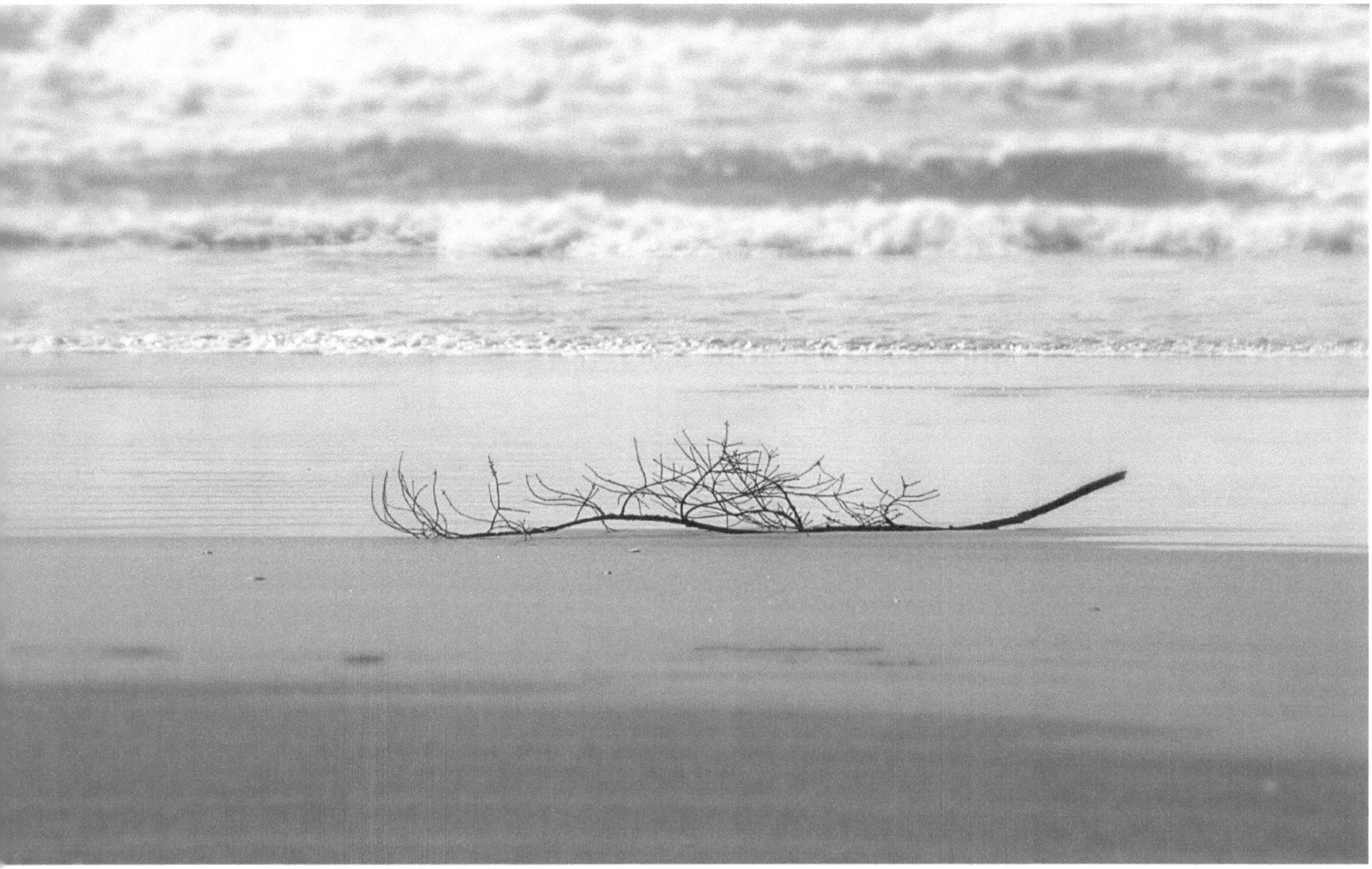

Above -'*Drifter*'- Newport, Oregon - April 2015

'*Nature Makes Art*' - Newport, Oregon - April 2015

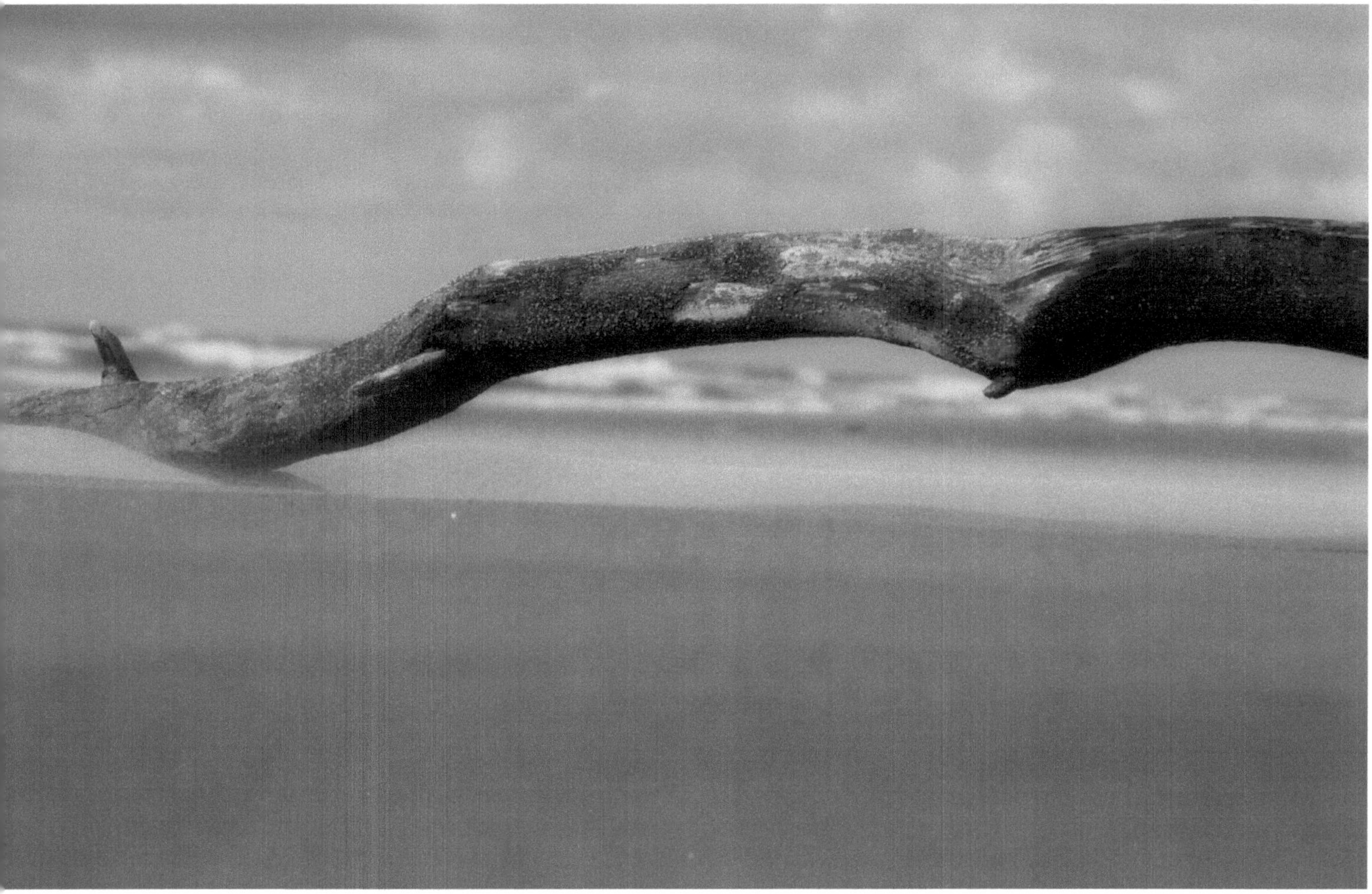

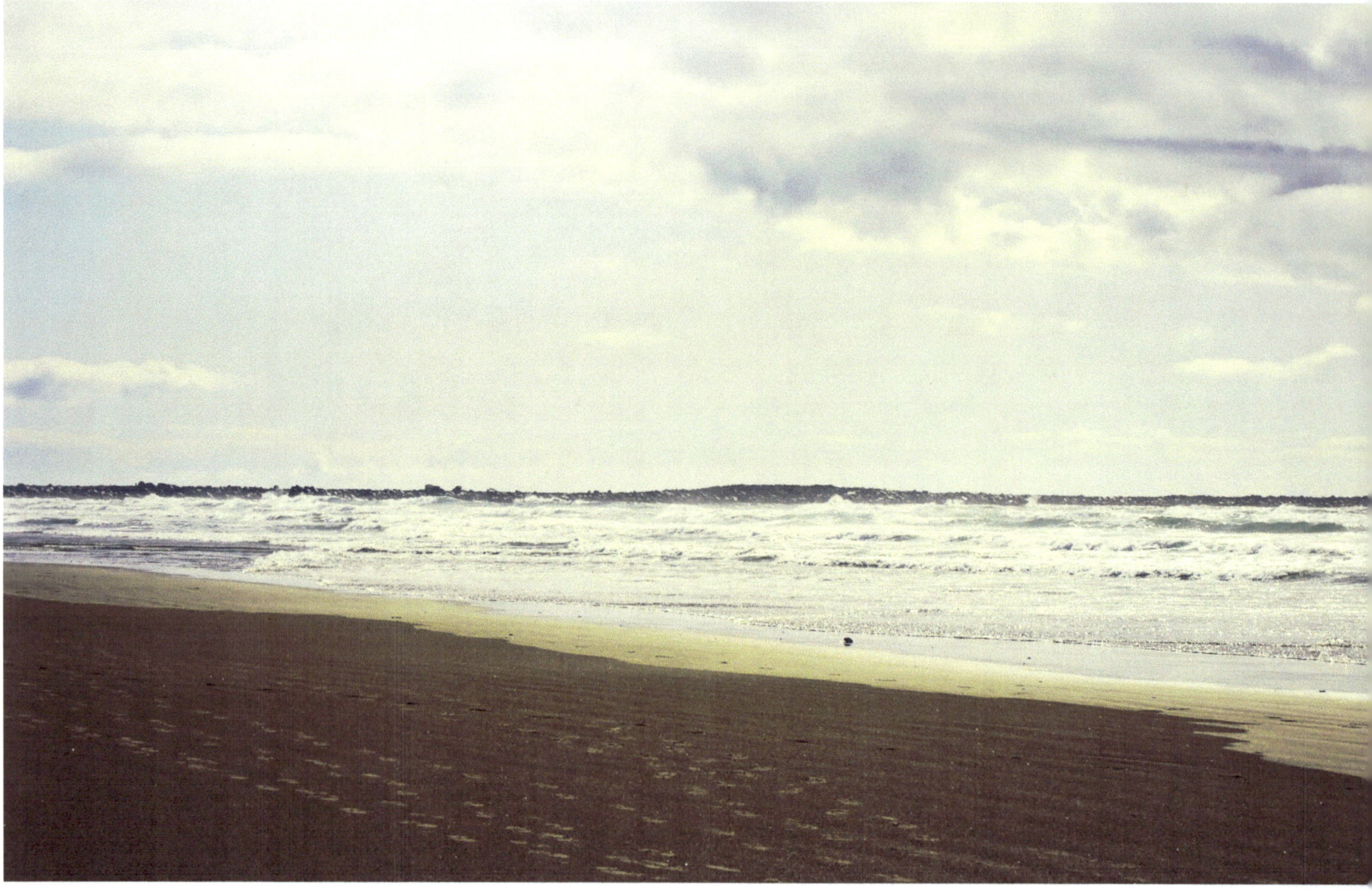

Above - *'Footprints On The Shore'* -Newport, Oregon 2015 - **Below -** *'Glorious Sounds'*

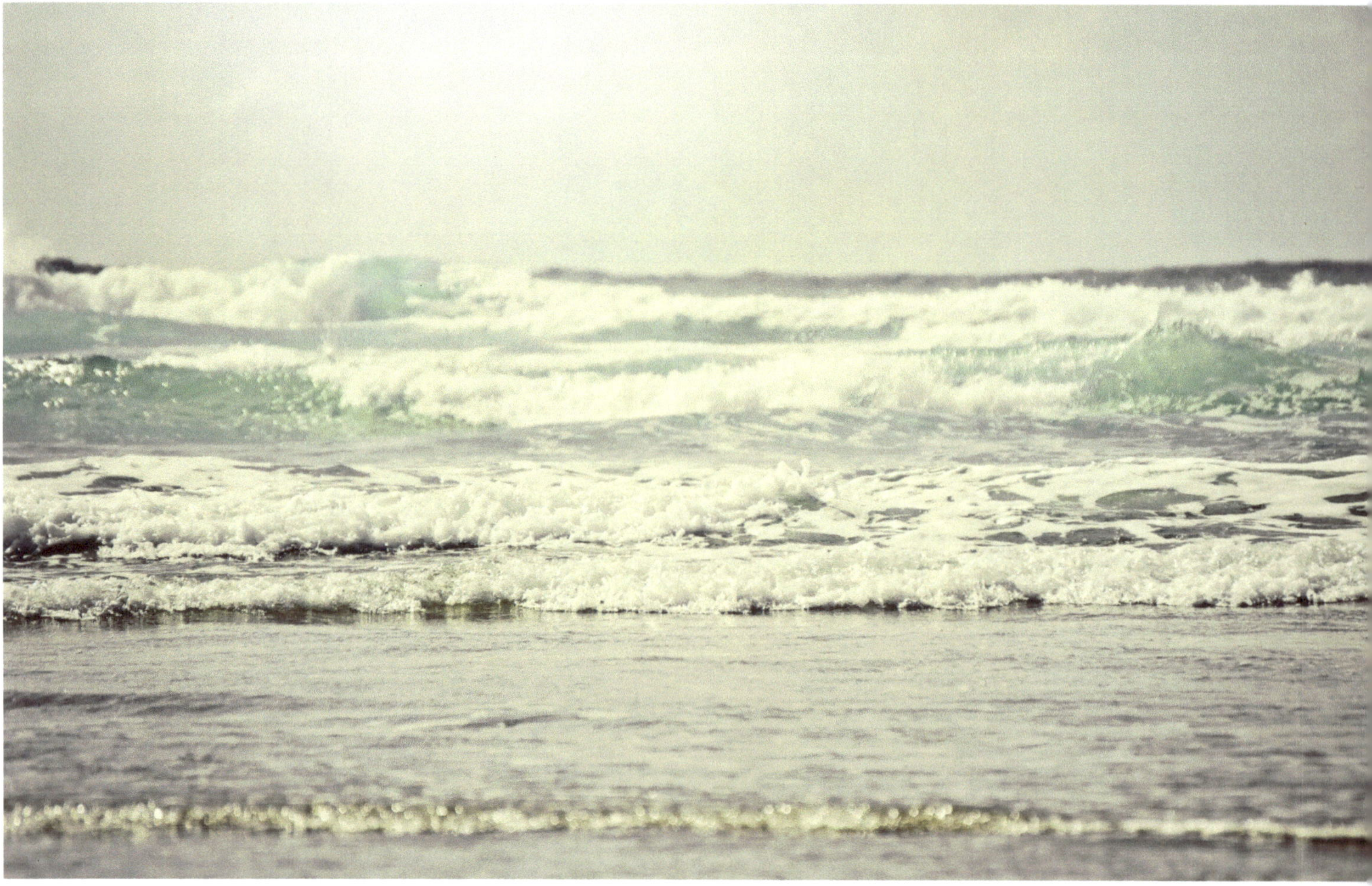

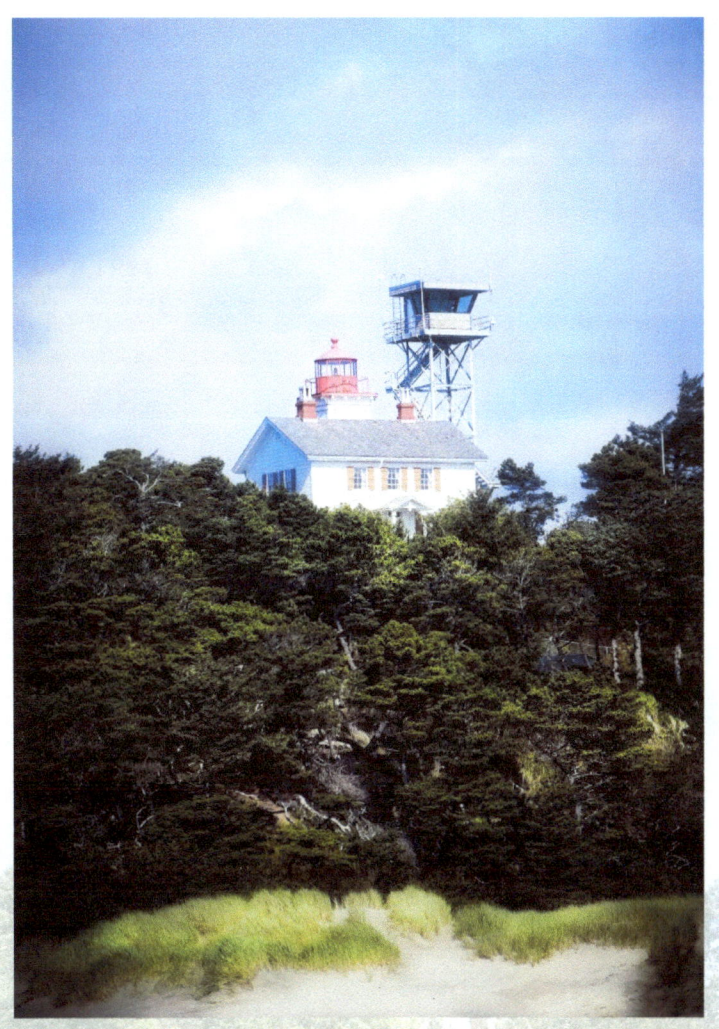

Yaquina Bay Lighthouse, which is located in the Yaquina Bay State Recreation Park. The bay is the most populated port between San Fransisco and Puget Sound. - Newport, Oregon 2015

There is nothing more serene and calming than the sight and sound of the ocean. The tide inching it's way up the shore and rolling waves. Being at the beach gives me a calm refreshed feeling. A feeling of being closer to everything. Closer to the sky and heaven above and closer to another way of life. I guess you could say the ocean is inspiring if you open your mind to it. It creates lasting memories in your heart and soul.

'Path To Destiny'

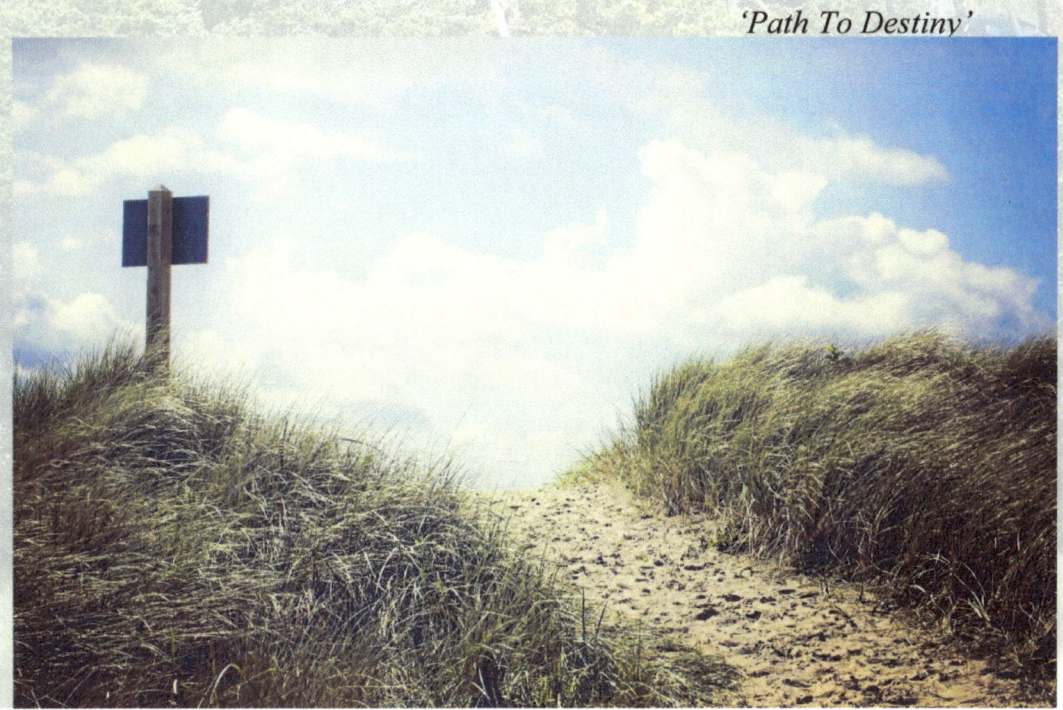

'Entrancing' - Sunset in Seeley Lake - 2015

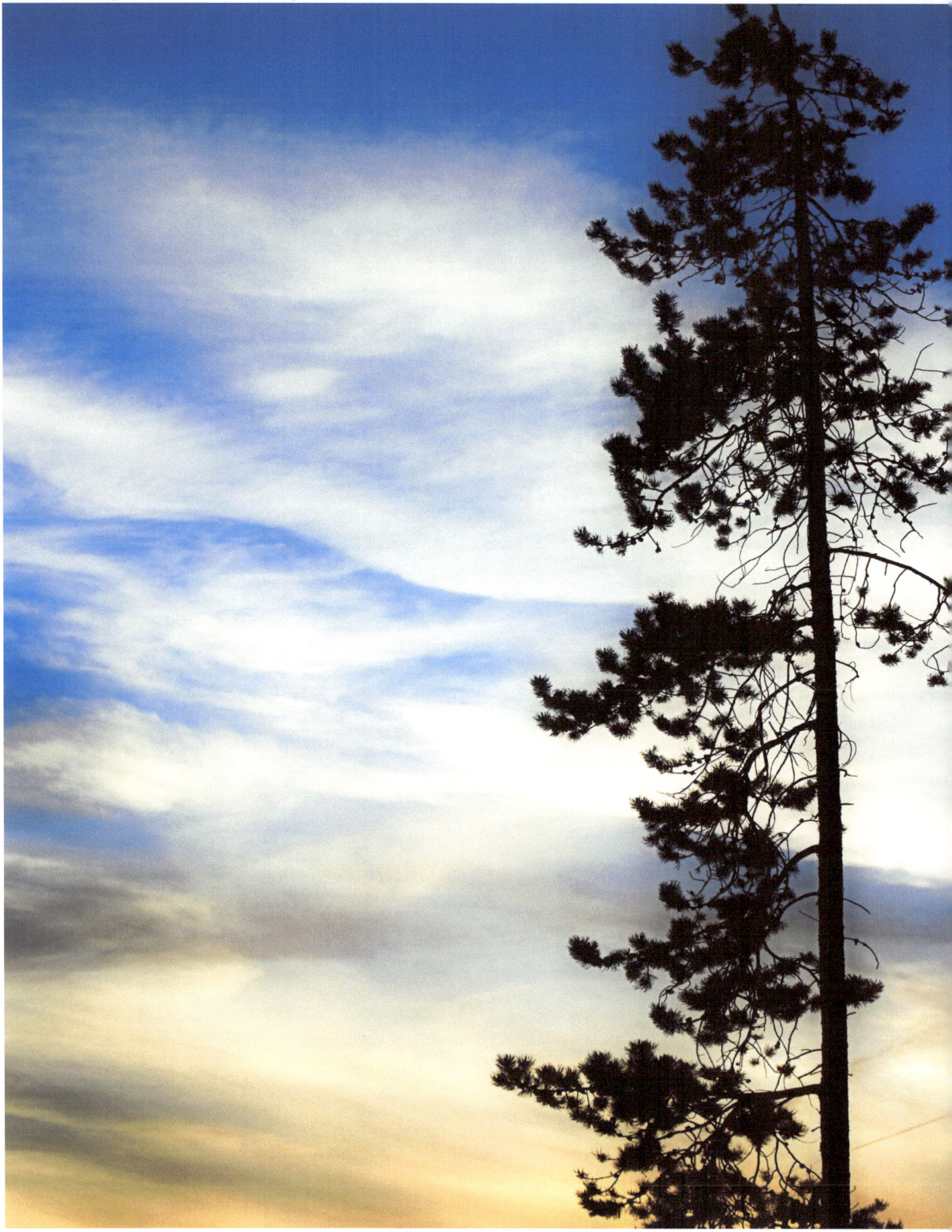

Right - *'Sunset Collage'* - A combination of three images. A sunset, the moon and lillies, creating an off set reality in a surrealistic dreamy vision.

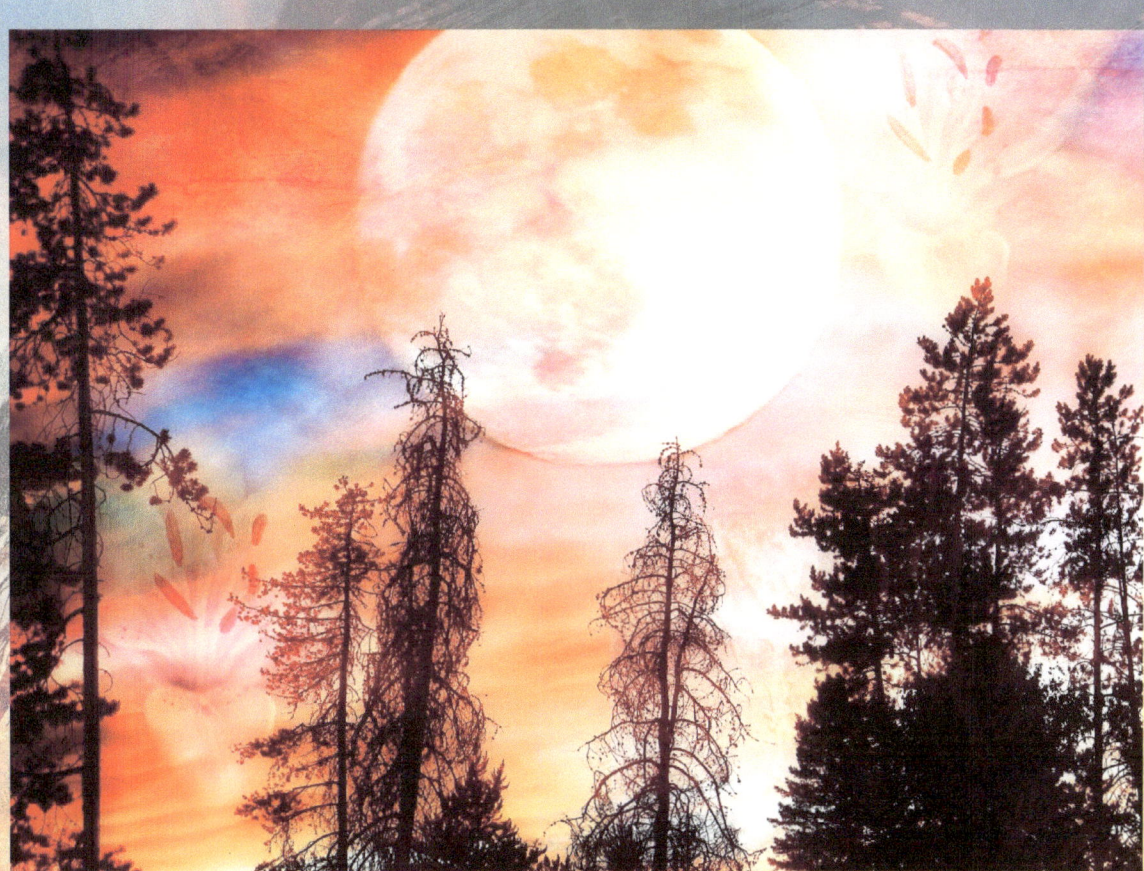

Both of these sunset images were created from several images of a beautiful sunset one evening from my porch in Seeley Lake, Montana

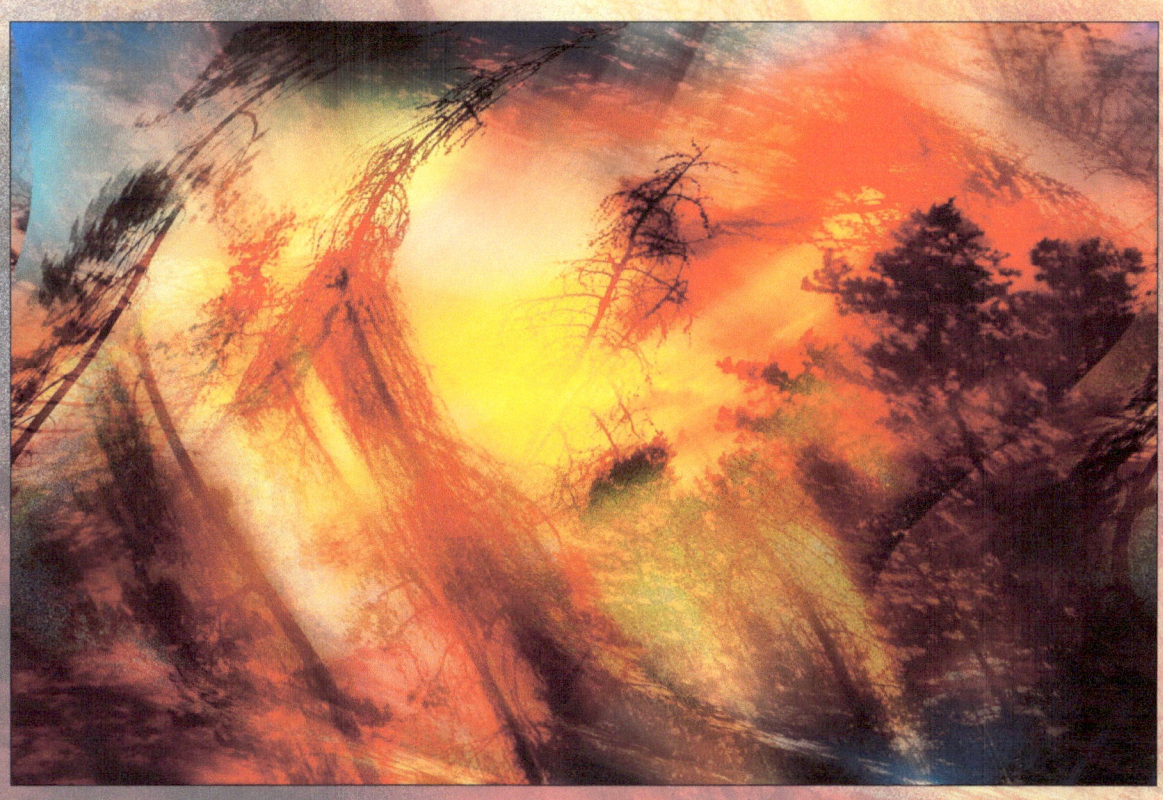

Left - *'Twisted Lemonade'* - Was created from an image entitled *'After The Storm'*. The colors already looked like lemonade in the sky, so I twisted and manipulated the scene making the color stand out and distorting the trees.

'Soul And Snowflakes' - Winter - Montana 2016

The life of a snowflake is short. The beautiful and the fascinating wonders of winter. As with everything in life, they have a story.

'Snowflake Life'

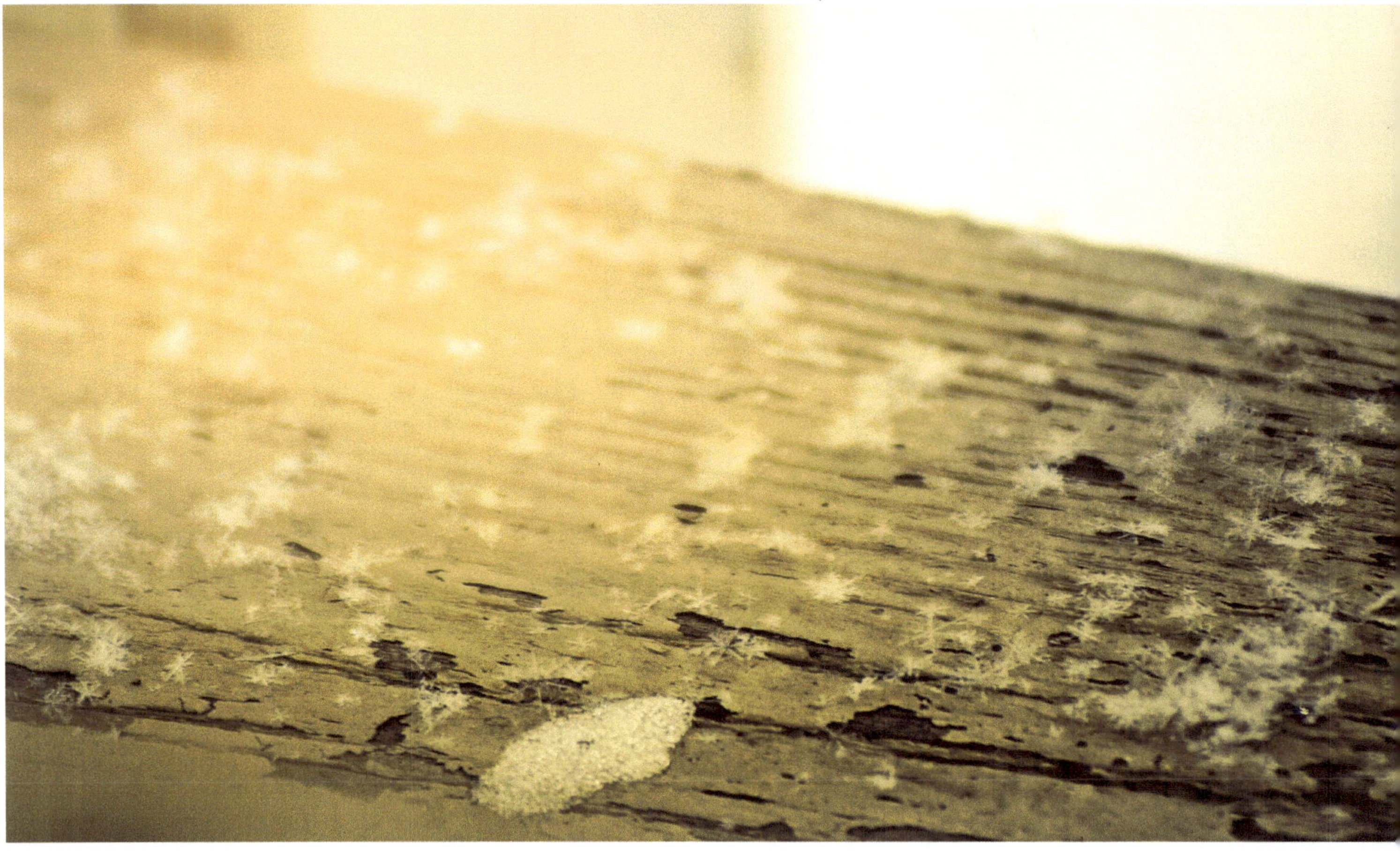

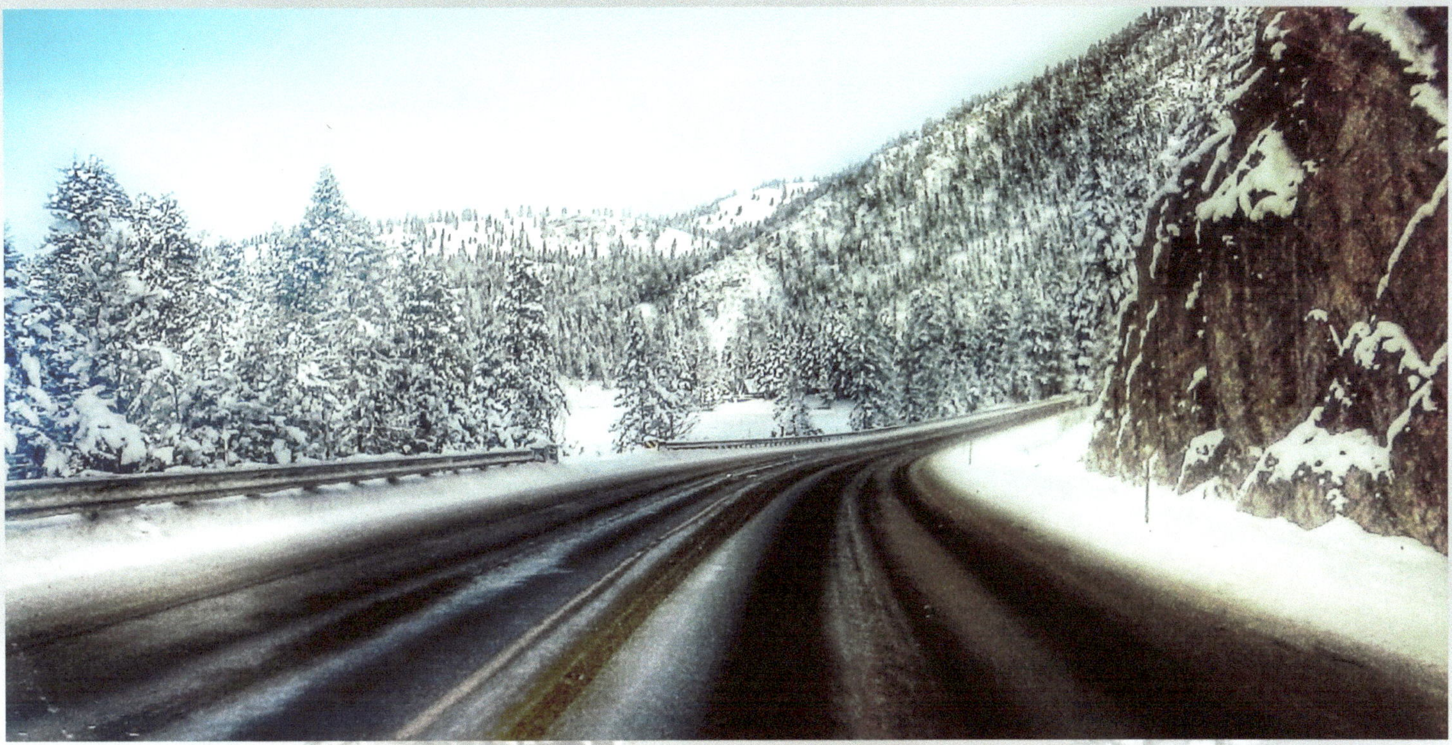

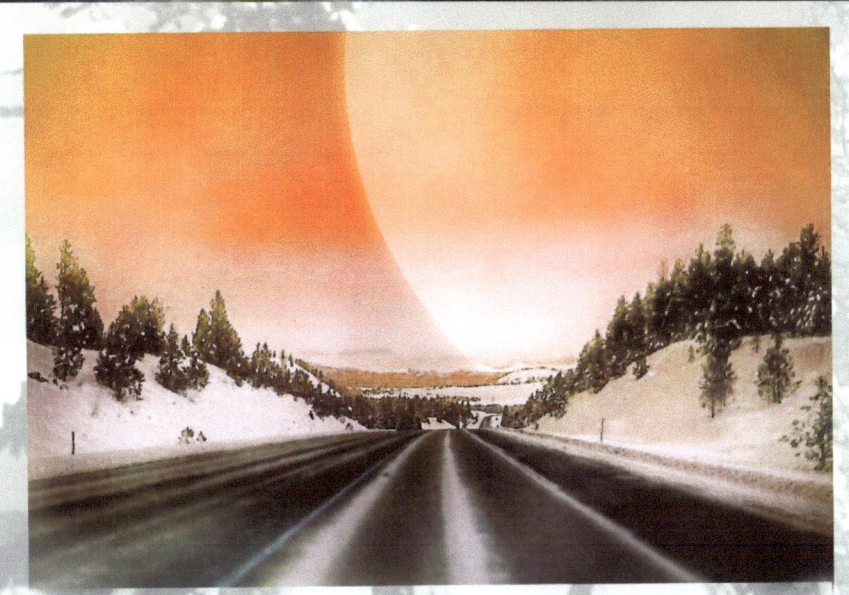

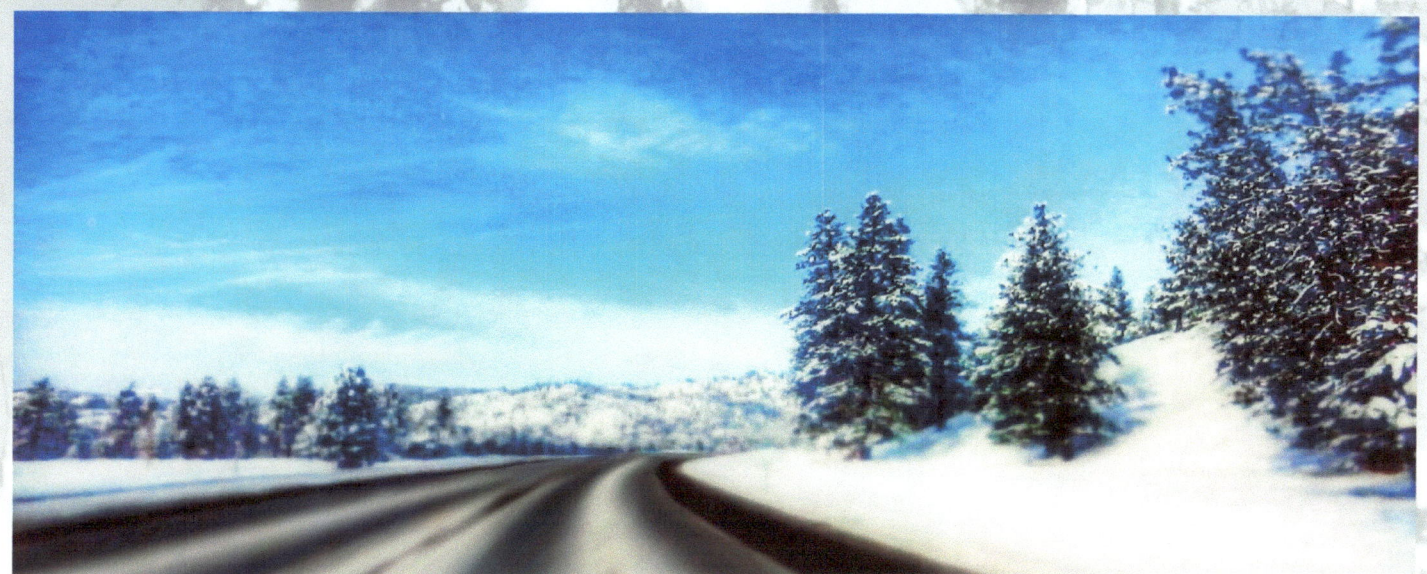

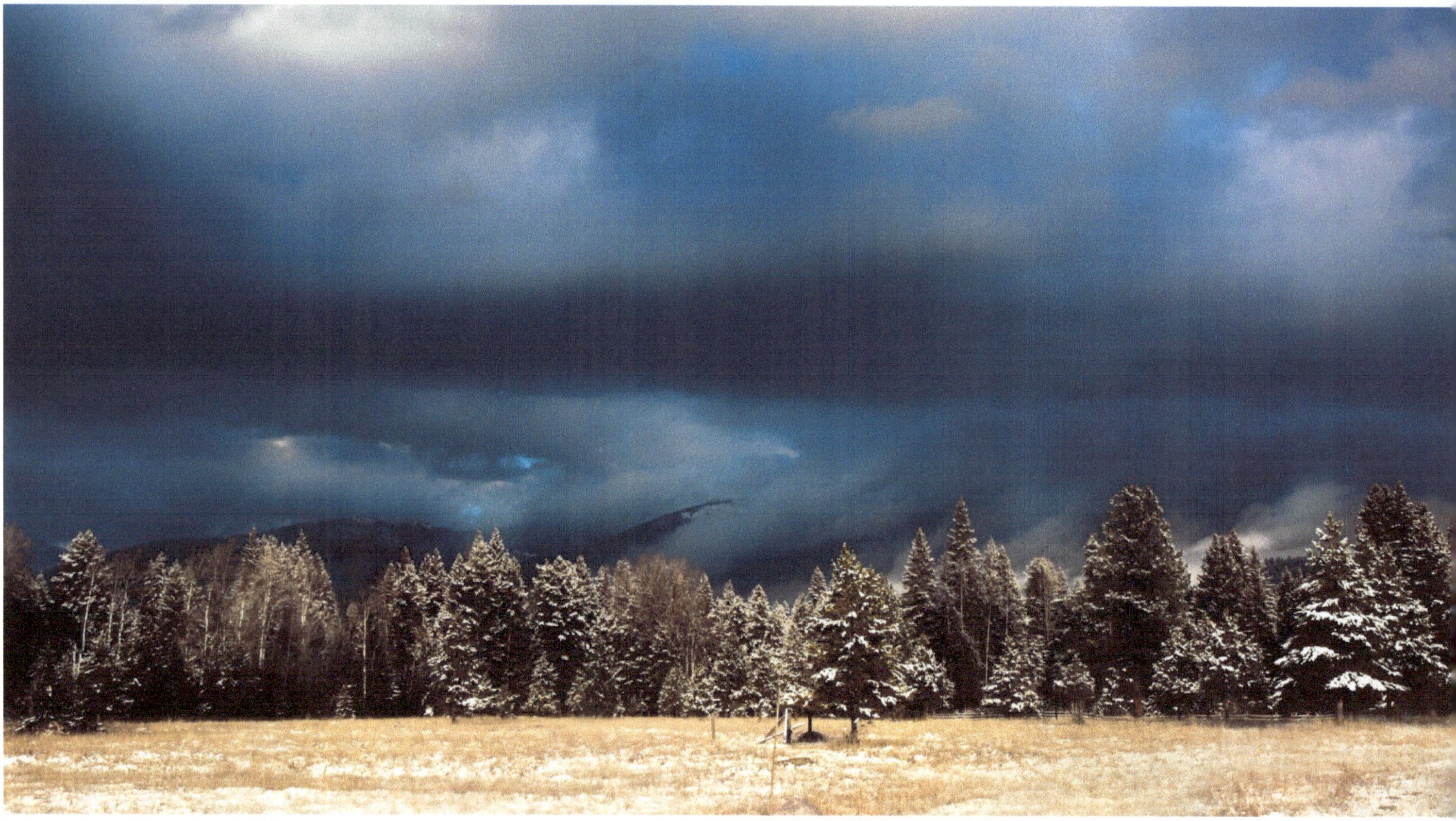

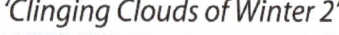

"Clinging Clouds of Winter'

   Both of these images taken in three seperate exposures and merged together. Taken at what locals call 'The Homestead' where a lot of people book weddings, reunions, ect. Part of the Double Arrow Ranch in Seeley Lake, Montana 2015 - Winter

'Clinging Clouds of Winter 2'

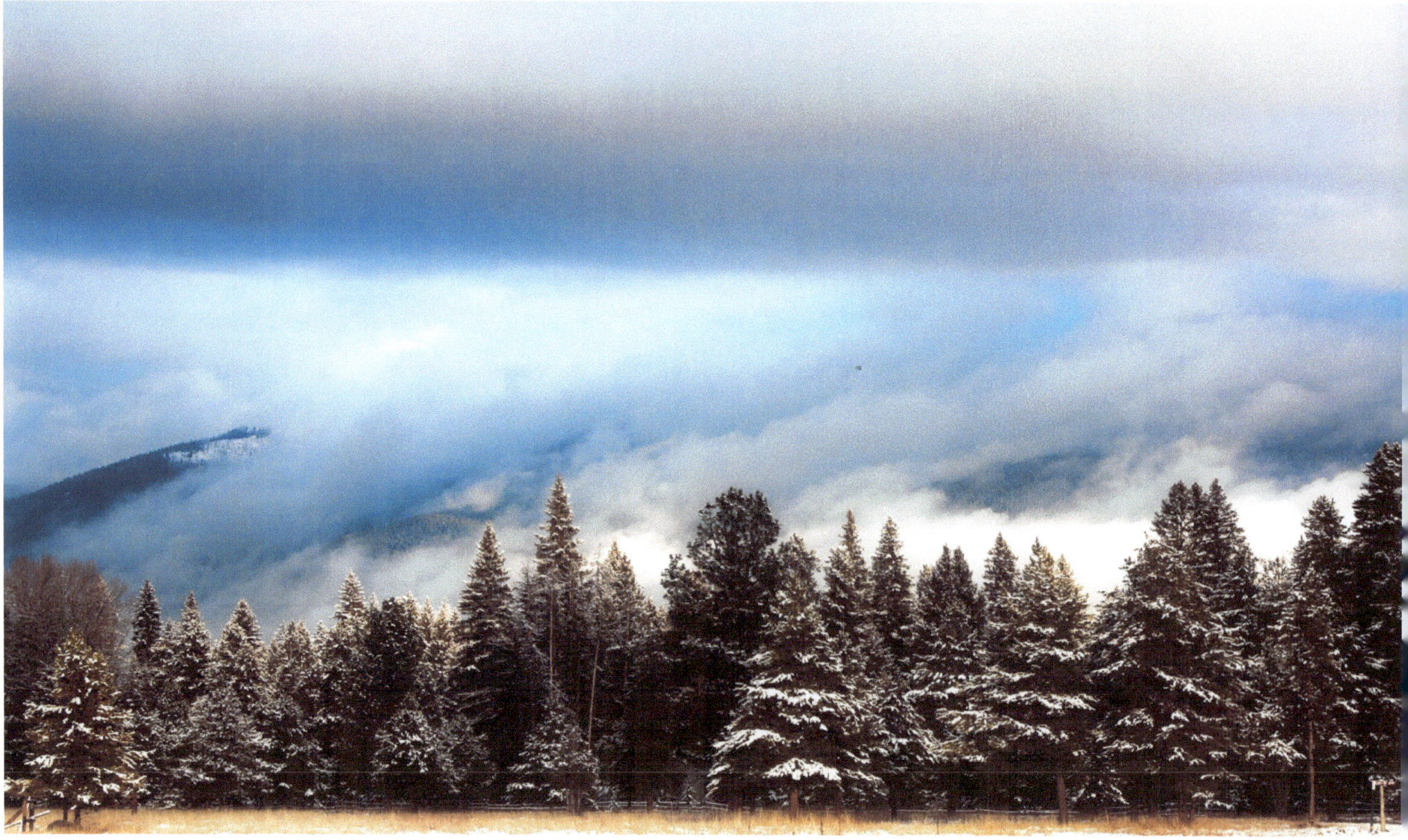

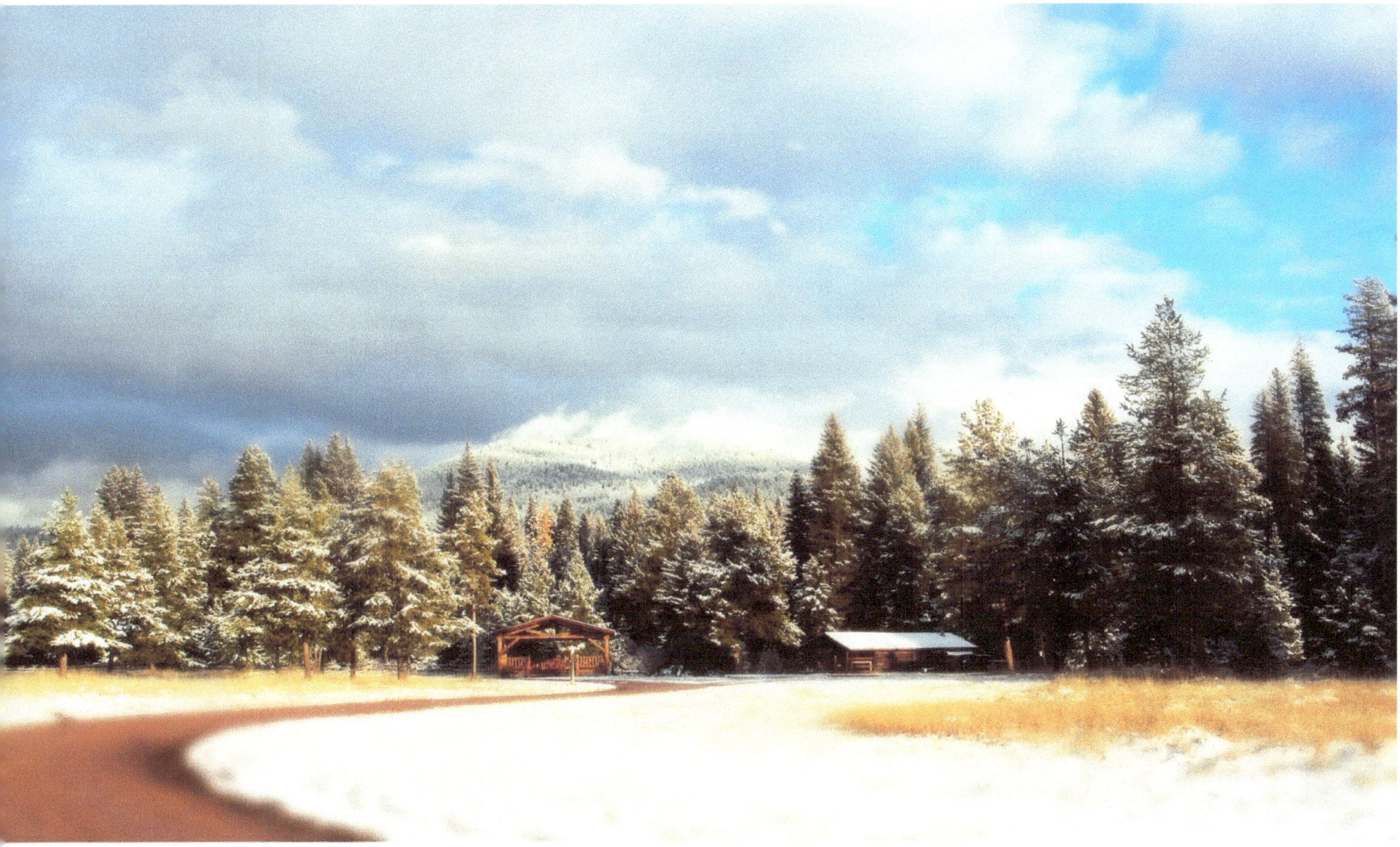

'Snow At The Homefront' '- Seeley Lake, Montana - 2015

Frosty Trees' -a multiple exposure imaged merged together. Seeley Lake Montana- 2016

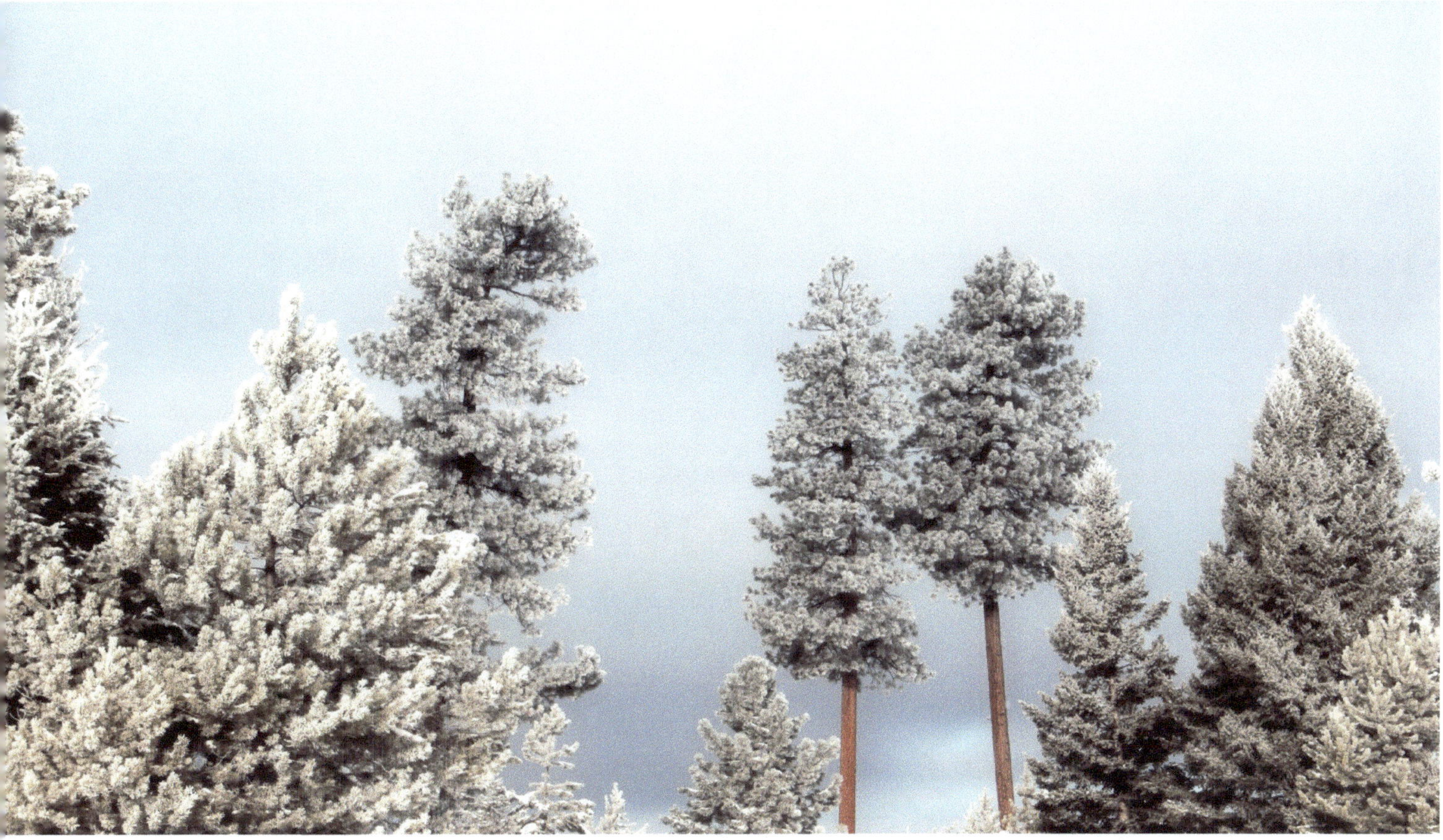

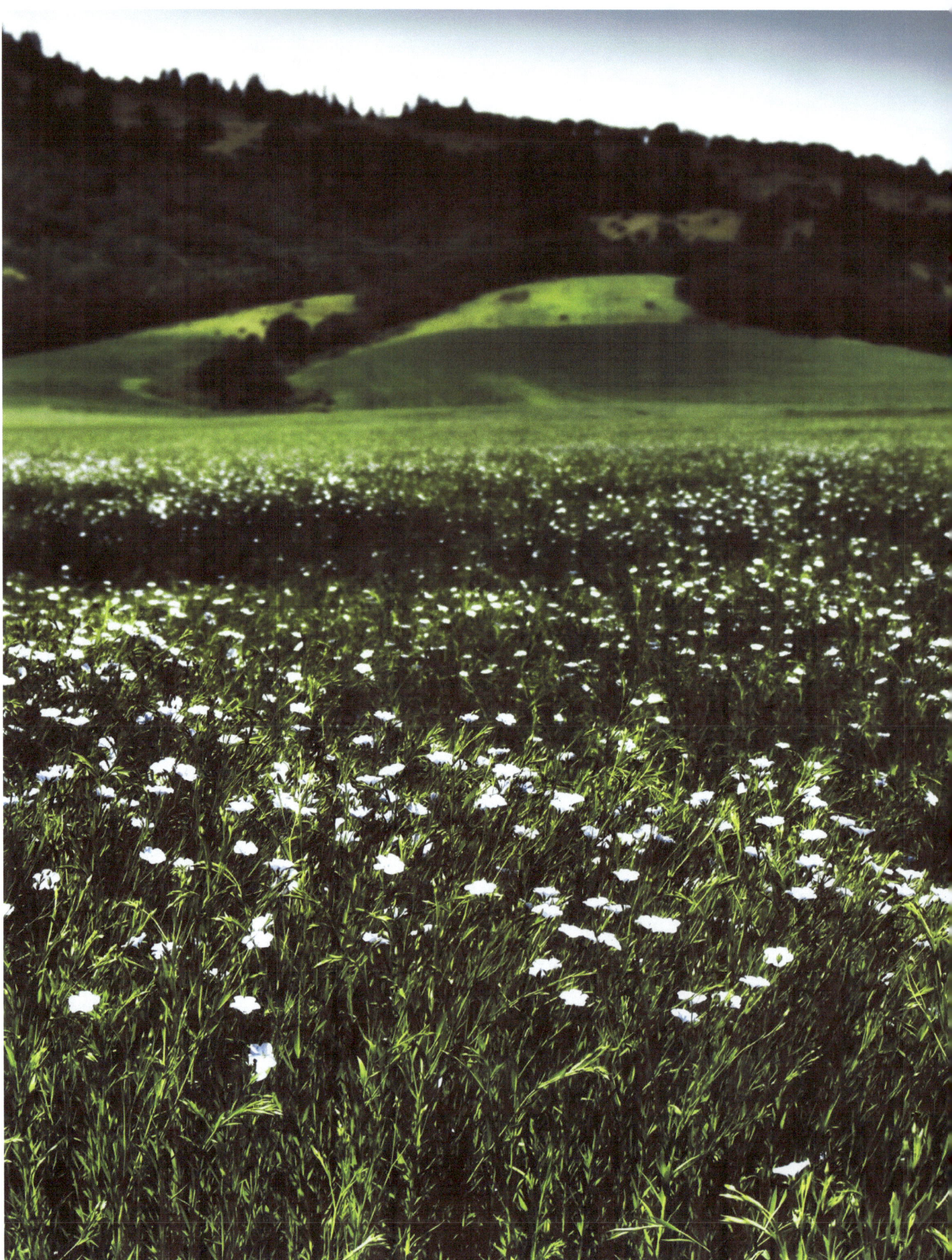

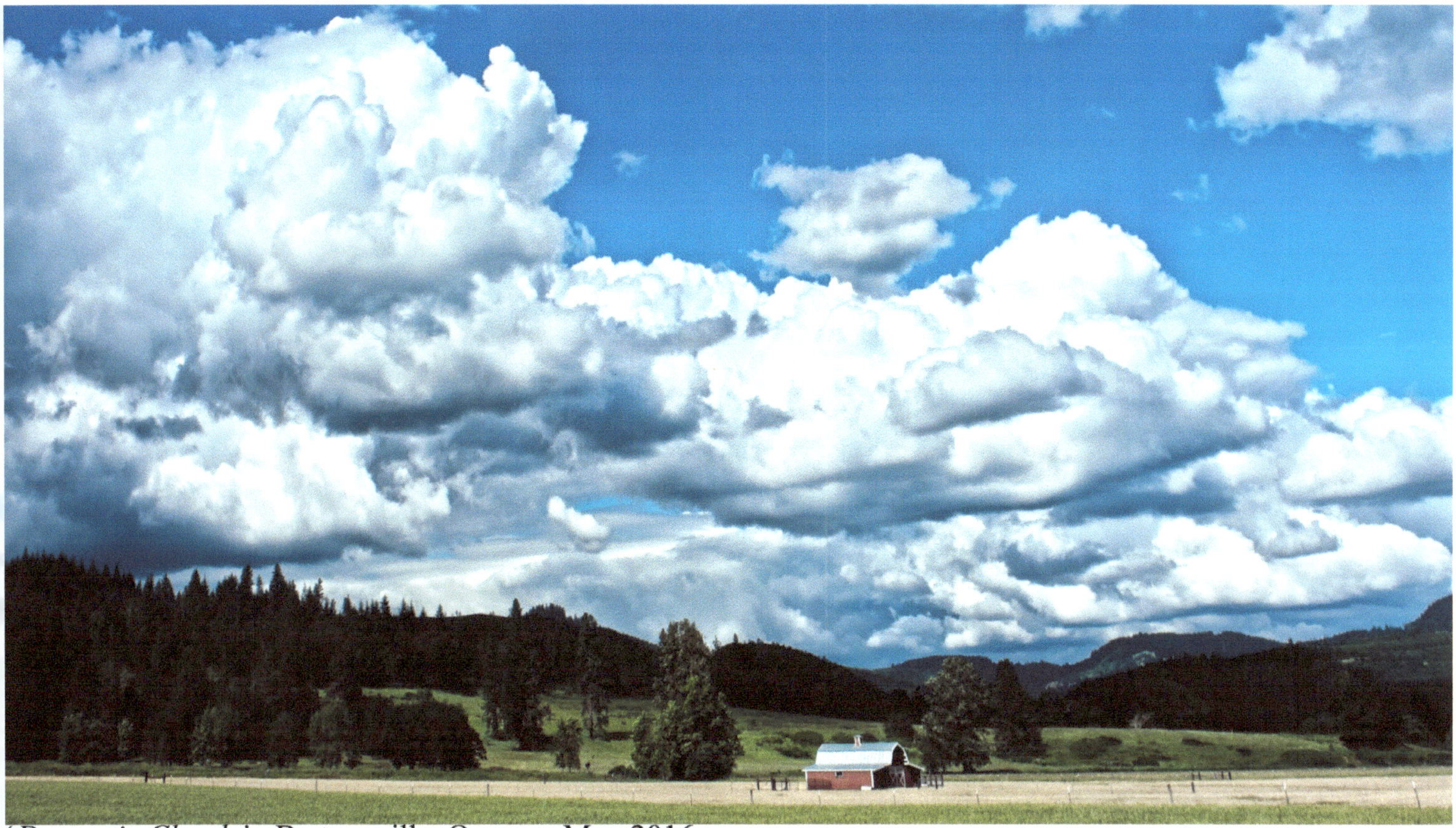

'*Dramatic Clouds*' - Brownsville, Oregon- May 2016

'*Peaceful Morning*' - Halsey, Oregon - May 2016

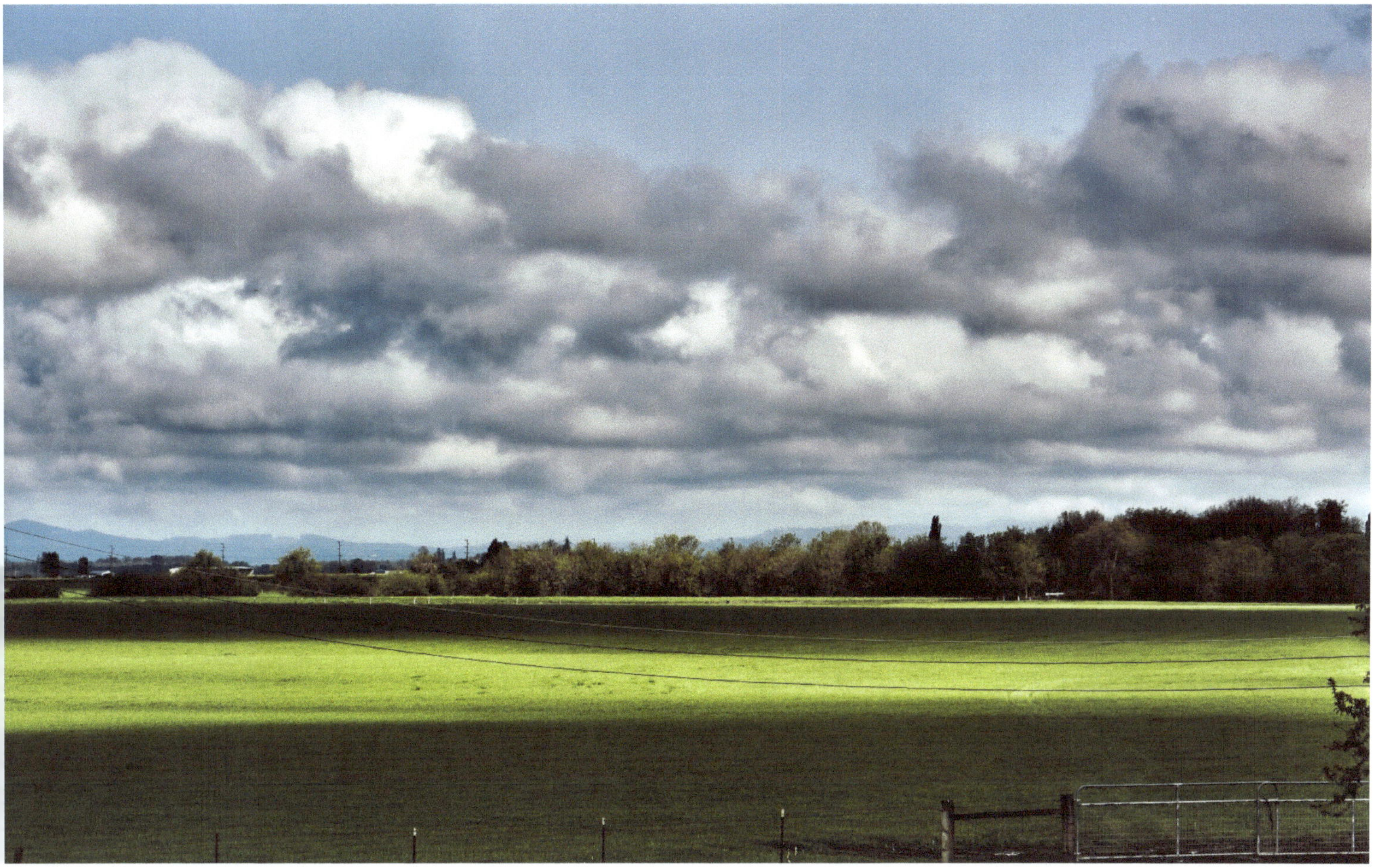

'Light It Up' - Rainbow Portrait -Halsey, Oregon - April 2016

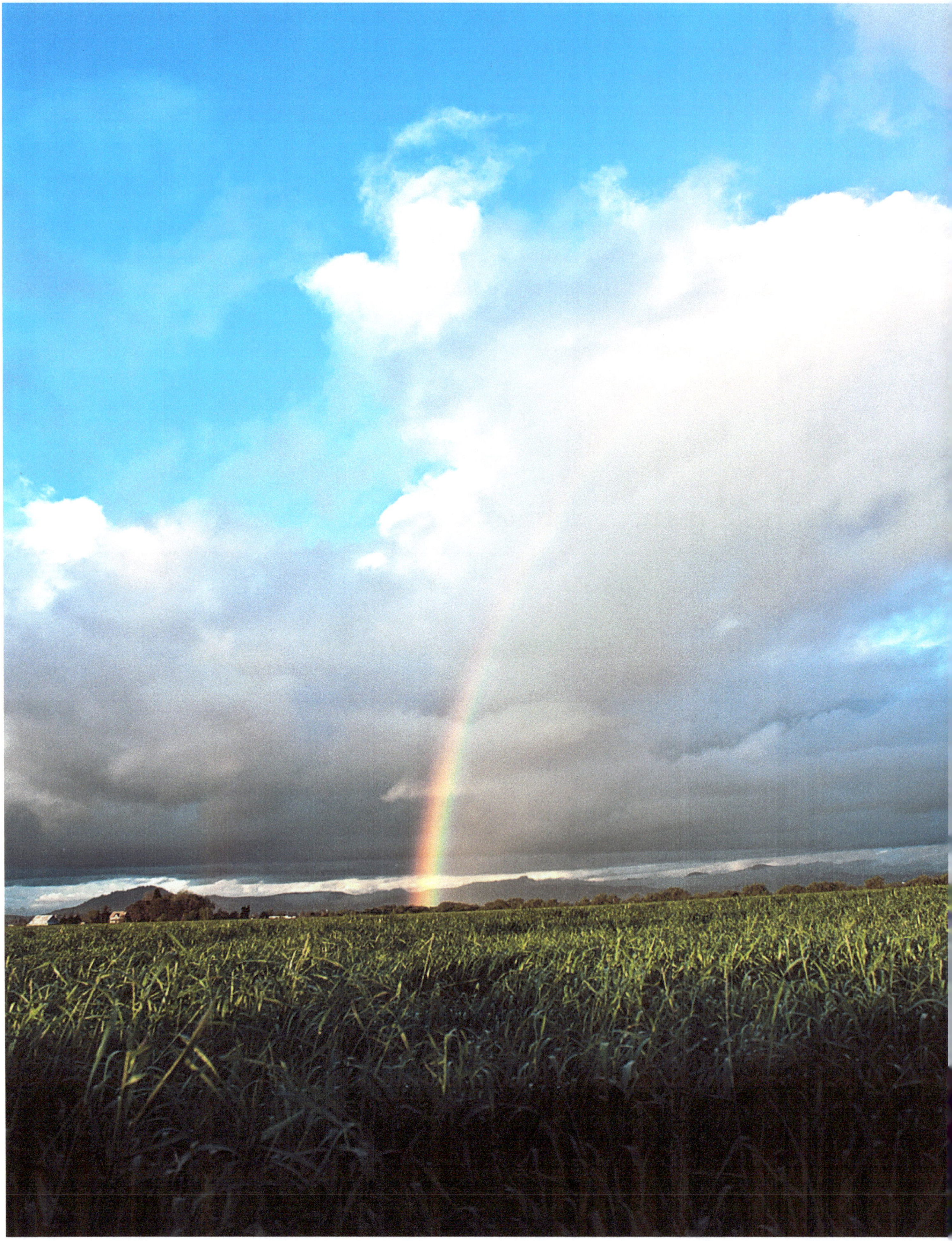

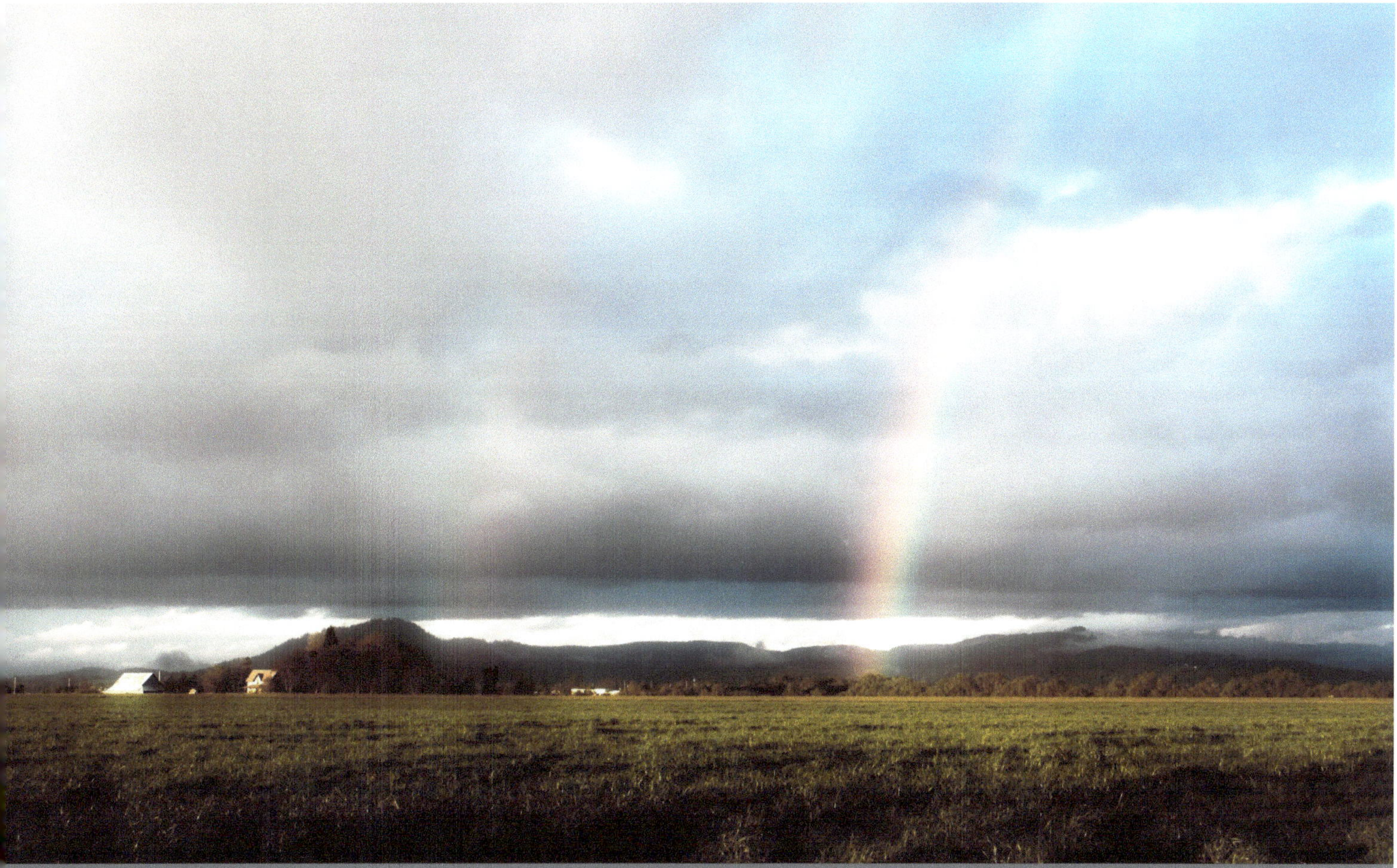

"After every storm, there is a rainbow. If you have eyes, you will find it. If you have wisdom, you will create it. If you have love for yourself and others, you won't need it." ~ Shannon L. Alder

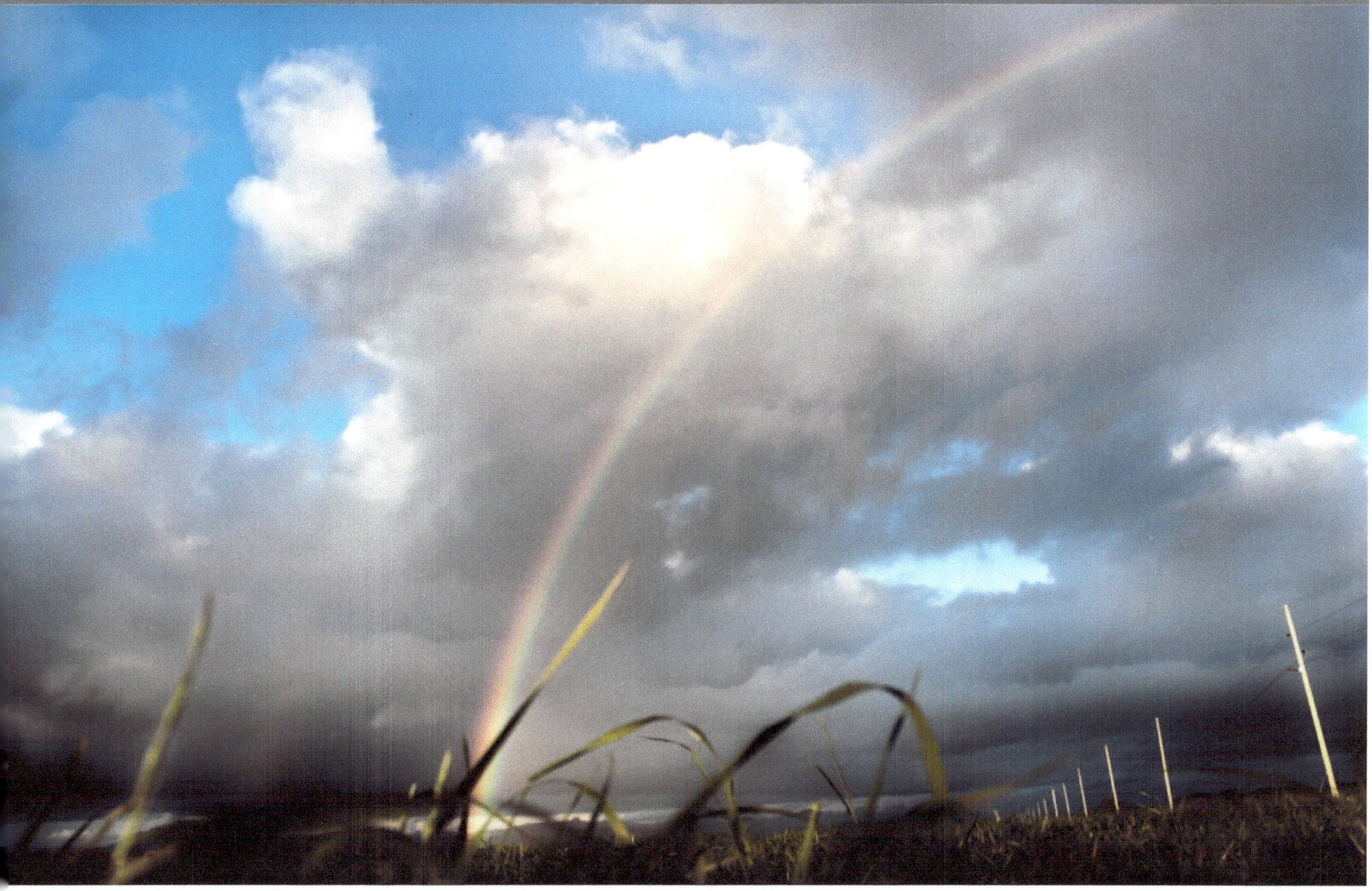

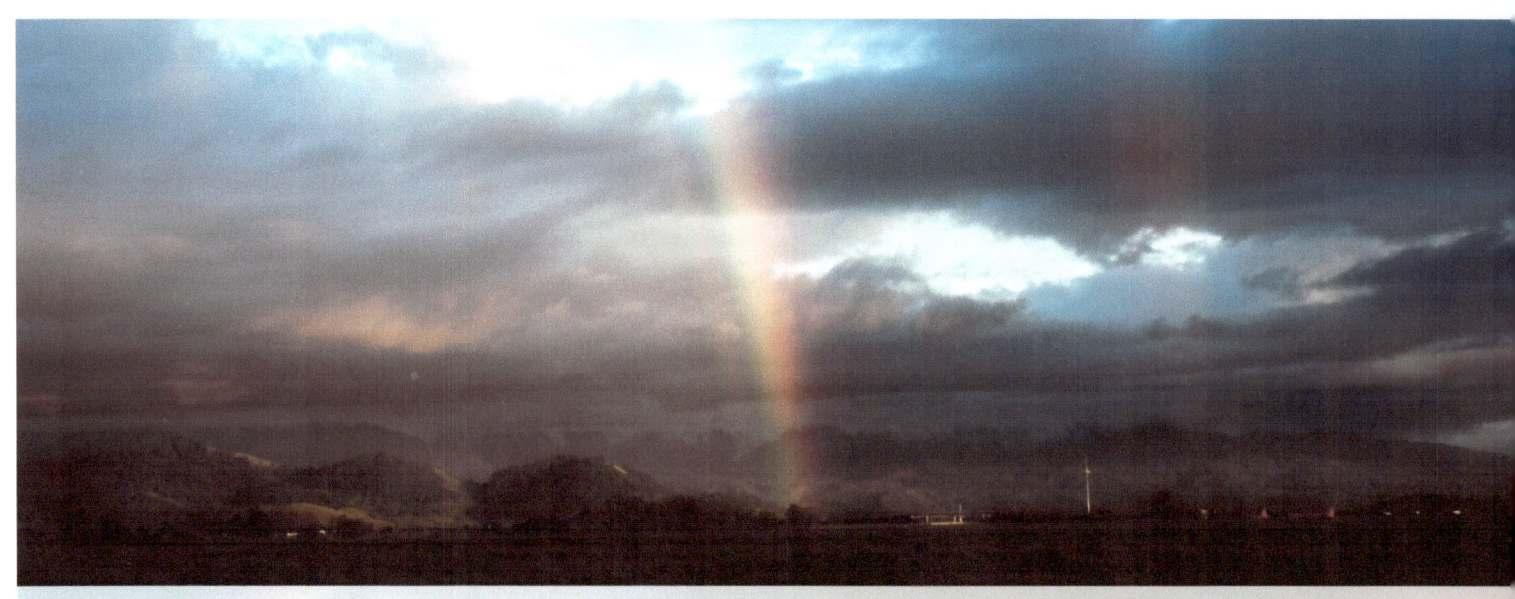

'Sunset Rainbow' - Halsey, Oregon area - April 2016

'Under The Rainbow' -Halsey, Oregon - June 2016

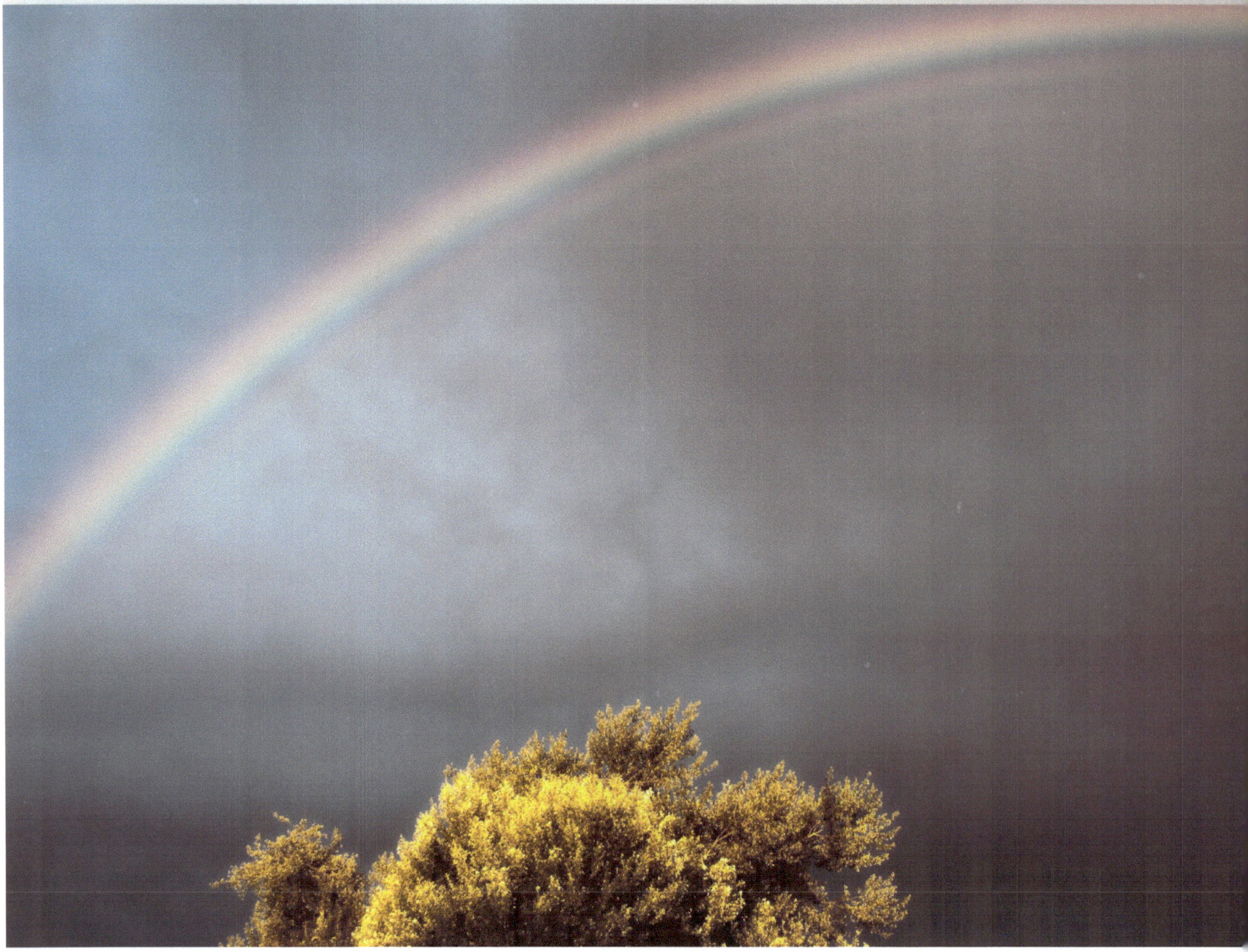

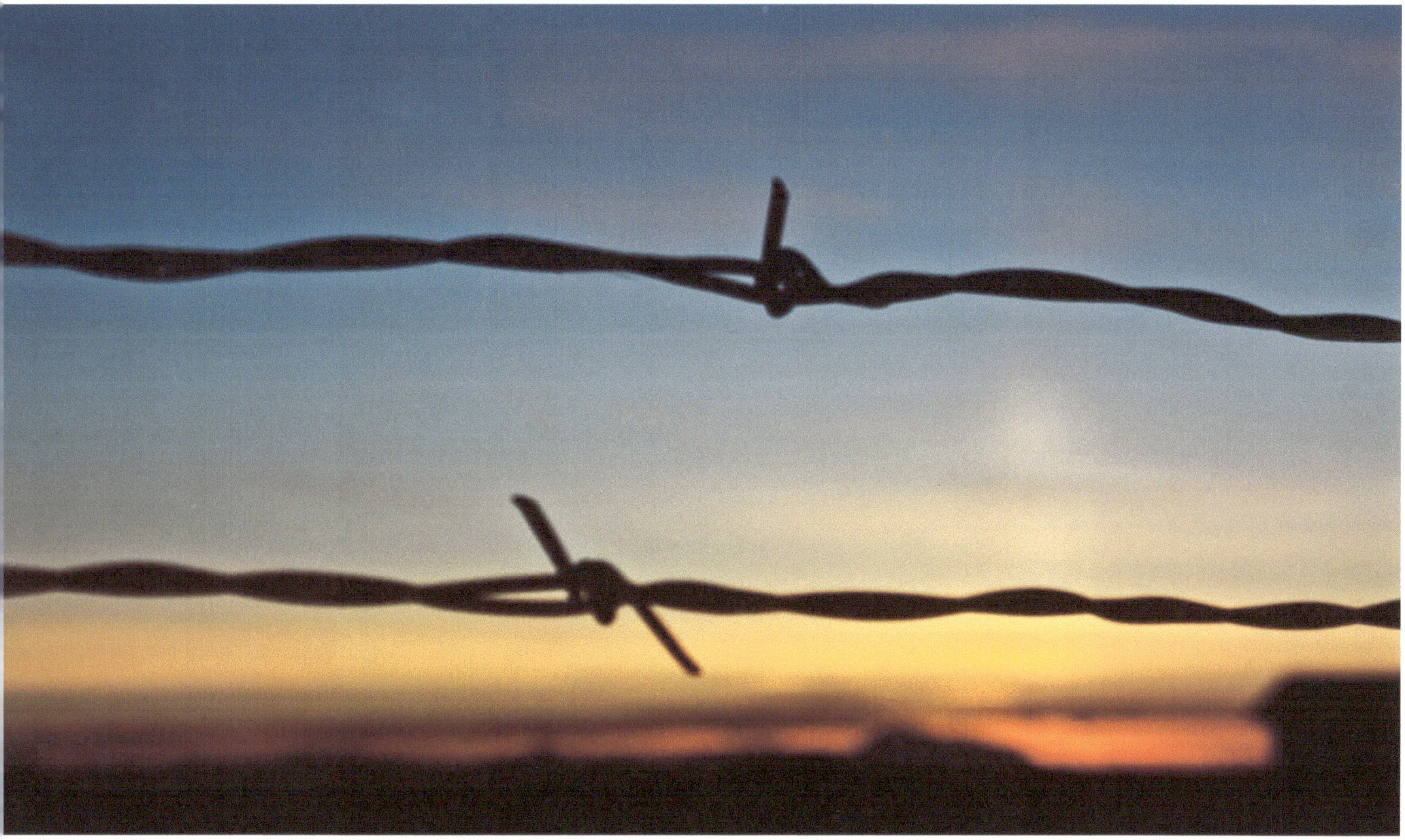

'Country Sunset' - Halsey, Oregon- May 2016

Every sunset symbolizes the day coming to an end. Each day being as different as the sunset. There is always something to make it different, whether it be good or not so good. Key aspects exist in the both - change and time.

'It Always Comes To A Different End'-Halsey, Oregon- May 2016

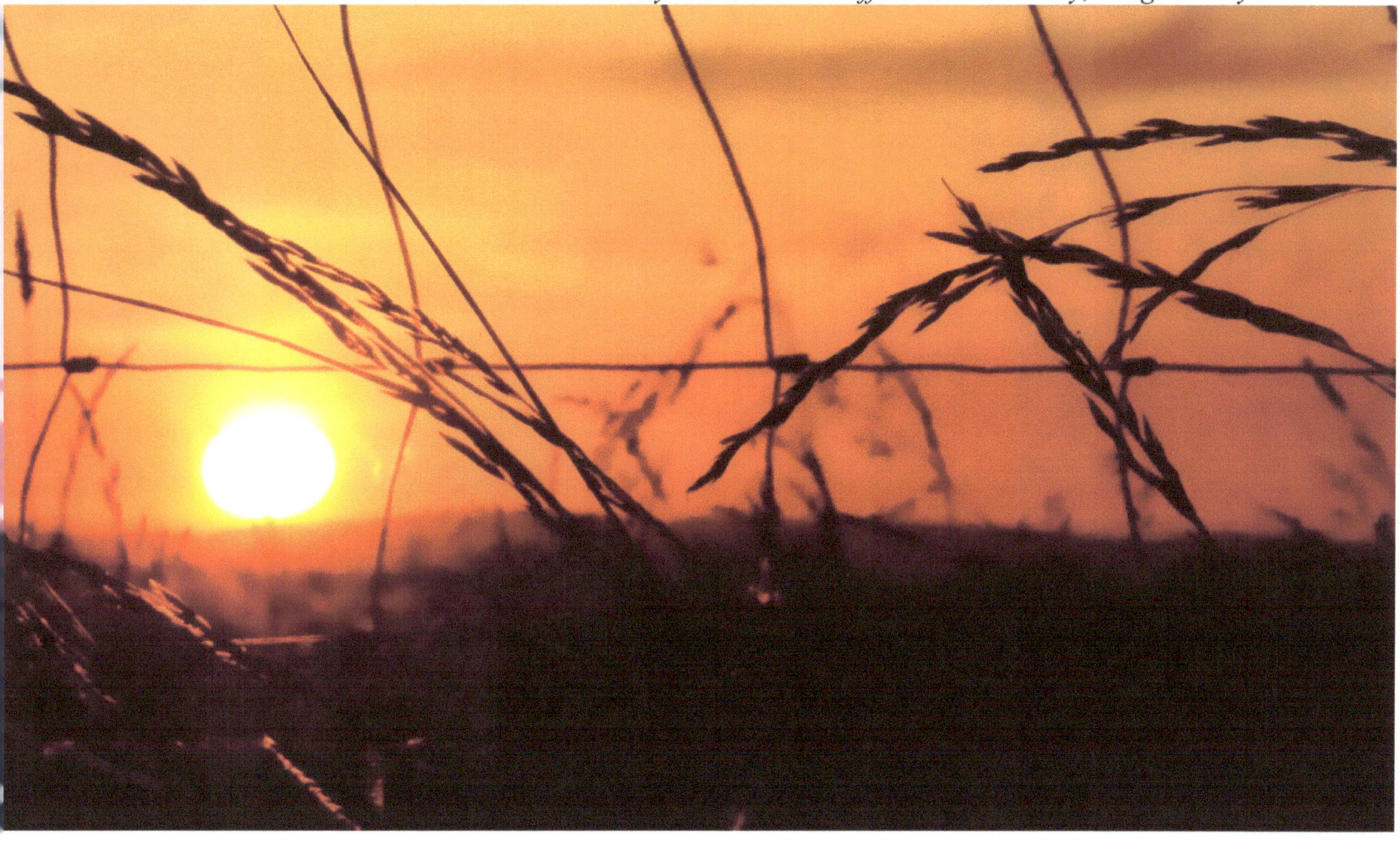

Introducción

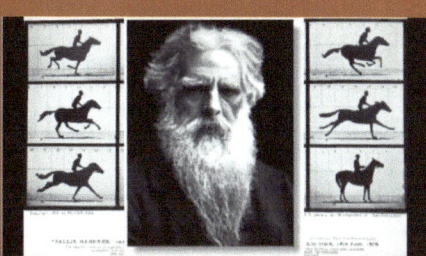

Panamá ha cambiado y la forma más dramática de realizarlo es mediante una comparación de las imágenes de cómo era "antes" y cómo es "ahora". Claro, a veces resulta más fácil decirlo que hacerlo. Algunos monumentos, edificios, calles, paraderos o estructuras ya no existen, otros son de acceso restringido y, en algunos casos, los peligros son tan grandes que se podría perder la vida en el intento de fotografiarlos. No obstante, la satisfacción de hallar un lugar histórico previamente investigado, la toma de una buena imagen, su edición y la verificación correspondiente, mitiga cualquier dificultad, sacrificio o riesgo.

En esta publicación, las imágenes del Panamá de Ayer (en blanco y negro) exhiben un breve título, con su texto original en inglés, lo que permite conocer cómo eran llamados estos sitios o sus alrededores en 1875. Hay que destacar que el fotógrafo fue muy hábil en la combinación de los diferentes aspectos de sus negativos (placas) para formar fotos individuales compuestas. Esto significa que los cielos o nubes de una imagen pueden aparecer en las fotos de los otros países visitados. Las imágenes del Panamá de Hoy (a colores) fueron captadas entre los meses de junio y septiembre de 2015. El encabezado presenta el nombre actual de la edificación, monumento o ubicación.

La serie de publicaciones anuales del "Ayer y Hoy" en Panamá inicia en el año 2008 y se basa en los principios de la refotografía, es decir, el acto de repetir una fotografía de un mismo sitio con un espacio de tiempo entre las dos imágenes. Este libro se enfoca en el trabajo de un importante, aunque enigmático, fotógrafo del siglo XIX: Eadweard Muybridge. Se espera que las fotografías de esta edición, captadas con 140 años de diferencia, fomenten el conocimiento, conservación y correcta restauración de nuestro patrimonio histórico.

Eadweard Muybridge, seudónimo de Edward James Muggeridge (1830 - 1904) fue un fotógrafo e investigador británico. Cambió su nombre cuando emigró a los Estados Unidos en 1851. Sus experimentos sobre la cronofotografía sirvieron de base para el posterior invento del cinematógrafo.

Comenzó trabajando en la encuadernación y venta de libros. Más tarde se interesó en la fotografía y, en 1860, aprendió sobre el proceso del colodión húmedo. En 1867, se dio a la tarea de registrar el escenario del lejano oeste. Produjo notables vistas estereoscópicas y más tarde panoramas, incluyendo series importantes sobre la ciudad de San Francisco.

En febrero de 1875, justo después de haber sido absuelto por el asesinato del amante de su mujer, abordó un buque de la Pacific Mail Steamship Company en San Francisco y viajó por América Central con el nombre de Eduardo Santiago Muybridge. Fotografió los países atendidos por la compañía naviera con la expectativa de que las fotografías fomentarían el turismo y las oportunidades de inversión por los magníficos paisajes presentados. A su regreso a California, en 1876, produjo y publicó aproximadamente once álbumes fotográficos que vendió o regaló

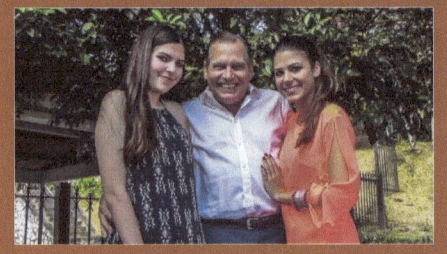

Jaime Massot Hernández. Nacido en Panamá el 19 de noviembre de 1959 con raíces españolas por parte de su madre Carmen Cristina Hernández Claramunt y su padre Juan José Massot Pellisé.

Su educación la recibió en varios colegios de la ciudad de Panamá (La Salle, Instituto Pedagógico y Javier). Es ingeniero civil egresado de la Universidad Santa María La Antigua (USMA) con estudios de postgrado (Hidrología) en Madrid (España) y maestrías en Letras (Summa Cum Laude / Administración de Empresas) y Ciencias (Magna Cum Laude / Administración Industrial) de la USMA.

Tiene 35 años de labores en el Canal de Panamá y ha ejercido funciones de supervisión y gerencia en adición a labores especializadas como hidrólogo, ingeniero civil e industrial, profesor universitario, fotógrafo, historiador, etc. Coordinó el Proyecto de Preservación de la Documentación Histórica del Canal de Panamá y dirige las actividades de la biblioteca del Club Unión de Panamá desde el 2000. Es miembro del Comité de Fotografía desde 1984.

Sus publicaciones tienen como propósito la creación, fomento, desarrollo y promoción de programas, proyectos y actividades que resalten la identidad nacional y el patrimonio cultural del conjunto monumental histórico de Panamá.

Índice